Automation Readiness
Complete Self-Assessment Guide

The guidance in this Self-Assessment is based on Automation Readiness best practices and standards in business process architecture, design and quality management. The guidance is also based on the professional judgment of the individual collaborators listed in the Acknowledgments.

Notice of rights

Trademarks

Table of Contents

About The Art of Service

The Art of Service, Business Process Architects since 2000, is dedicated to helping stakeholders achieve excellence.

Defining, designing, creating, and implementing a process to solve a stakeholders challenge or meet an objective is the most valuable role… In EVERY group, company, organization and department.

Unless you're talking a one-time, single-use project, there should be a process. Whether that process is managed and implemented by humans, AI, or a combination of the two, it needs to be designed by someone with a complex enough perspective to ask the right questions.

Someone capable of asking the right questions and step back and say, 'What are we really trying to accomplish here? And is there a different way to look at it?'

With The Art of Service's Standard Requirements Self-Assessments, we empower people who can do just that — whether their title is marketer, entrepreneur, manager, salesperson, consultant, Business Process Manager, executive assistant, IT Manager, CIO etc... —they are the people who rule the future. They are people who watch the process as it happens, and ask the right questions to make the process work better.

Contact us when you need any support with this Self-Assessment and any help with templates, blue-prints and examples of standard documents you might need:

http://theartofservice.com
service@theartofservice.com

Acknowledgments

This checklist was developed under the auspices of The Art of Service, chaired by Gerardus Blokdyk.

Representatives from several client companies participated in the preparation of this Self-Assessment.

In addition, we are thankful for the design and printing services provided.

Included Resources - how to access

Included with your purchase of the book is the Automation Readiness Self-Assessment Spreadsheet Dashboard which contains all questions and Self-Assessment areas and auto-generates insights, graphs, and project RACI planning - all with examples to get you started right away.

How? Simply send an email to
access@theartofservice.com
with this books' title in the subject to get the Automation Readiness Self Assessment Tool right away.

You will receive the following contents with New and Updated specific criteria:

- The latest quick edition of the book in PDF

- The latest complete edition of the book in PDF, which criteria correspond to the criteria in...

- The Self-Assessment Excel Dashboard, and...

- Example pre-filled Self-Assessment Excel Dashboard to get familiar with results generation

- In-depth specific Checklists covering the topic

- Project management checklists and templates to assist with implementation

INCLUDES LIFETIME SELF ASSESSMENT UPDATES

Every self assessment comes with Lifetime Updates and Lifetime Free Updated Books. Lifetime Updates is an industry-first feature which allows you to receive verified self assessment updates, ensuring you always have the most accurate information at your fingertips.

Get it now- you will be glad you did - do it now, before you forget.

Send an email to **access@theartofservice.com** with this books' title in the subject to get the Automation Readiness Self Assessment Tool right away.

Your feedback is invaluable to us

If you recently bought this book, we would love to hear from you! You can do this by writing a review on amazon (or the online store where you purchased this book) about your last purchase! As part of our continual service improvement process, we love to hear real client experiences and feedback.

How does it work?
To post a review on Amazon, just log in to your account and click on the Create Your Own Review button (under Customer Reviews) of the relevant product page. You can find examples of product reviews in Amazon. If you purchased from another online store, simply follow their procedures.

What happens when I submit my review?
Once you have submitted your review, send us an email at review@theartofservice.com with the link to your review so we can properly thank you for your feedback.

Purpose of this Self-Assessment

This Self-Assessment has been developed to improve understanding of the requirements and elements of Automation Readiness, based on best practices and standards in business process architecture, design and quality management.

It is designed to allow for a rapid Self-Assessment to determine how closely existing management practices and procedures correspond to the elements of the Self-Assessment.

The criteria of requirements and elements of Automation Readiness have been rephrased in the format of a Self-Assessment questionnaire, with a seven-criterion scoring system, as explained in this document.

In this format, even with limited background knowledge of

Automation Readiness, a manager can quickly review existing operations to determine how they measure up to the standards. This in turn can serve as the starting point of a 'gap analysis' to identify management tools or system elements that might usefully be implemented in the organization to help improve overall performance.

How to use the Self-Assessment

On the following pages are a series of questions to identify to what extent your Automation Readiness initiative is complete in comparison to the requirements set in standards.

To facilitate answering the questions, there is a space in front of each question to enter a score on a scale of '1' to '5'.

1 Strongly Disagree

2 Disagree

3 Neutral

4 Agree

5 Strongly Agree

Read the question and rate it with the following in front of mind:

**'In my belief,
the answer to this question is clearly defined'.**

There are two ways in which you can choose to interpret this statement;
1. how aware are you that the answer to the question is clearly defined
2. for more in-depth analysis you can choose to gather

evidence and confirm the answer to the question. This obviously will take more time, most Self-Assessment users opt for the first way to interpret the question and dig deeper later on based on the outcome of the overall Self-Assessment.

A score of '1' would mean that the answer is not clear at all, where a '5' would mean the answer is crystal clear and defined. Leave emtpy when the question is not applicable or you don't want to answer it, you can skip it without affecting your score. Write your score in the space provided.

After you have responded to all the appropriate statements in each section, compute your average score for that section, using the formula provided, and round to the nearest tenth. Then transfer to the corresponding spoke in the Automation Readiness Scorecard on the second next page of the Self-Assessment.

Your completed Automation Readiness Scorecard will give you a clear presentation of which Automation Readiness areas need attention.

Automation Readiness Scorecard Example

Example of how the finalized Scorecard can look like:

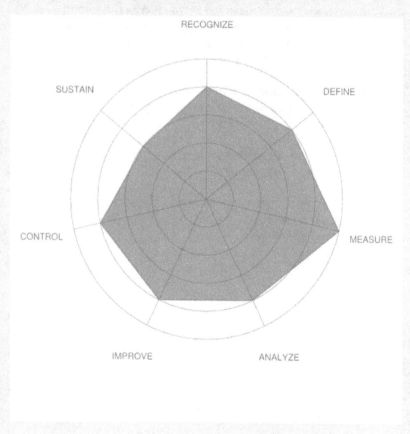

Automation Readiness Scorecard

Your Scores:

BEGINNING OF THE SELF-ASSESSMENT:

CRITERION #1: RECOGNIZE

INTENT: Be aware of the need for change. Recognize that there is an unfavorable variation, problem or symptom.

In my belief, the answer to this question is clearly defined:

5 Strongly Agree

4 Agree

3 Neutral

2 Disagree

1 Strongly Disagree

1. How do you take a forward-looking perspective in identifying Automation Readiness research related to market response and models?
<--- Score

2. To what extent would your organization benefit from being recognized as a award recipient?
<--- Score

3. What is the recognized need?
<--- Score

4. Which needs are not included or involved?
<--- Score

5. Will Automation Readiness deliverables need to be tested and, if so, by whom?
<--- Score

6. Who needs to know about Automation Readiness?
<--- Score

7. What do employees need in the short term?
<--- Score

8. Why is this needed?
<--- Score

9. What information do users need?
<--- Score

10. How do you identify subcontractor relationships?
<--- Score

11. Will new equipment/products be required to facilitate Automation Readiness delivery, for example is new software needed?
<--- Score

12. Would you recognize a threat from the inside?
<--- Score

13. How are you going to measure success?
<--- Score

14. What vendors make products that address the Automation Readiness needs?

<--- Score

15. What are the stakeholder objectives to be achieved with Automation Readiness?

<--- Score

16. Why the need?

<--- Score

17. How do you recognize an objection?

<--- Score

18. Do you have/need 24-hour access to key personnel?

<--- Score

19. How much are sponsors, customers, partners, stakeholders involved in Automation Readiness? In other words, what are the risks, if Automation Readiness does not deliver successfully?

<--- Score

20. To what extent does each concerned units management team recognize Automation Readiness as an effective investment?

<--- Score

21. When a Automation Readiness manager recognizes a problem, what options are available?

<--- Score

22. What situation(s) led to this Automation Readiness Self Assessment?

<--- Score

23. Do you recognize Automation Readiness achievements?

<--- Score

24. What is the extent or complexity of the Automation Readiness problem?

<--- Score

25. What Automation Readiness events should you attend?

<--- Score

26. What else needs to be measured?

<--- Score

27. What problems are you facing and how do you consider Automation Readiness will circumvent those obstacles?

<--- Score

28. What do you need to start doing?

<--- Score

29. Who needs to know?

<--- Score

30. Who else hopes to benefit from it?

<--- Score

31. What are the clients issues and concerns?

<--- Score

32. Are employees recognized for desired behaviors?

<--- Score

33. Does your organization need more Automation Readiness education?

<--- Score

34. Is it clear when you think of the day ahead of you what activities and tasks you need to complete?

<--- Score

35. How do you assess your Automation Readiness workforce capability and capacity needs, including skills, competencies, and staffing levels?

<--- Score

36. Do you know what you need to know about Automation Readiness?

<--- Score

37. What would happen if Automation Readiness weren't done?

<--- Score

38. Are controls defined to recognize and contain problems?

<--- Score

39. Are there any specific expectations or concerns about the Automation Readiness team, Automation Readiness itself?

<--- Score

40. What tools and technologies are needed for a custom Automation Readiness project?

<--- Score

41. Is the quality assurance team identified?

<--- Score

42. What is the smallest subset of the problem you can usefully solve?
<--- Score

43. Have you identified your Automation Readiness key performance indicators?
<--- Score

44. Does the problem have ethical dimensions?
<--- Score

45. What extra resources will you need?
<--- Score

46. What are the timeframes required to resolve each of the issues/problems?
<--- Score

47. As a sponsor, customer or management, how important is it to meet goals, objectives?
<--- Score

48. Think about the people you identified for your Automation Readiness project and the project responsibilities you would assign to them, what kind of training do you think they would need to perform these responsibilities effectively?
<--- Score

49. How are the Automation Readiness's objectives aligned to the group's overall stakeholder strategy?
<--- Score

50. How can auditing be a preventative security

measure?

<--- Score

51. What Automation Readiness coordination do you need?

<--- Score

52. Did you miss any major Automation Readiness issues?

<--- Score

53. Are there recognized Automation Readiness problems?

<--- Score

54. What are your needs in relation to Automation Readiness skills, labor, equipment, and markets?

<--- Score

55. What needs to be done?

<--- Score

56. What activities does the governance board need to consider?

<--- Score

57. How many trainings, in total, are needed?

<--- Score

58. Who needs budgets?

<--- Score

59. Do you need to avoid or amend any Automation Readiness activities?

<--- Score

60. What training and capacity building actions are needed to implement proposed reforms?
<--- Score

61. Whom do you really need or want to serve?
<--- Score

62. What Automation Readiness problem should be solved?
<--- Score

63. What resources or support might you need?
<--- Score

64. Who defines the rules in relation to any given issue?
<--- Score

65. Are there Automation Readiness problems defined?
<--- Score

66. What creative shifts do you need to take?
<--- Score

67. Is it needed?
<--- Score

68. Where is training needed?
<--- Score

69. What does Automation Readiness success mean to the stakeholders?
<--- Score

70. Are there regulatory / compliance issues?

<--- Score

71. How does it fit into your organizational needs and tasks?
<--- Score

72. Who are your key stakeholders who need to sign off?
<--- Score

73. Are problem definition and motivation clearly presented?
<--- Score

74. Looking at each person individually – does every one have the qualities which are needed to work in this group?
<--- Score

75. Can management personnel recognize the monetary benefit of Automation Readiness?
<--- Score

76. How are training requirements identified?
<--- Score

77. What are the minority interests and what amount of minority interests can be recognized?
<--- Score

78. Does Automation Readiness create potential expectations in other areas that need to be recognized and considered?
<--- Score

79. Are you dealing with any of the same issues today

as yesterday? What can you do about this?
<--- Score

80. What prevents you from making the changes you know will make you a more effective Automation Readiness leader?
<--- Score

81. Do you need different information or graphics?
<--- Score

82. Will a response program recognize when a crisis occurs and provide some level of response?
<--- Score

83. How do you recognize an Automation Readiness objection?
<--- Score

84. What is the problem and/or vulnerability?
<--- Score

85. What is the problem or issue?
<--- Score

86. Consider your own Automation Readiness project, what types of organizational problems do you think might be causing or affecting your problem, based on the work done so far?
<--- Score

87. What should be considered when identifying available resources, constraints, and deadlines?
<--- Score

88. Is the need for organizational change recognized?

<--- Score

89. Which issues are too important to ignore?
<--- Score

90. Where do you need to exercise leadership?
<--- Score

91. Are losses recognized in a timely manner?
<--- Score

92. What are the expected benefits of Automation Readiness to the stakeholder?
<--- Score

93. What needs to stay?
<--- Score

94. Will it solve real problems?
<--- Score

95. Which information does the Automation Readiness business case need to include?
<--- Score

96. Are employees recognized or rewarded for performance that demonstrates the highest levels of integrity?
<--- Score

97. Who needs what information?
<--- Score

98. Are there any revenue recognition issues?
<--- Score

99. For your Automation Readiness project, identify and describe the business environment, is there more than one layer to the business environment?
<--- Score

100. Are your goals realistic? Do you need to redefine your problem? Perhaps the problem has changed or maybe you have reached your goal and need to set a new one?
<--- Score

Add up total points for this section:
_____ = Total points for this section

Divided by: _____ (number of statements answered) = _____
Average score for this section

Transfer your score to the Automation Readiness Index at the beginning of the Self-Assessment.

CRITERION #2: DEFINE:

INTENT: Formulate the stakeholder problem. Define the problem, needs and objectives.

In my belief, the answer to this question is clearly defined:

5 Strongly Agree

4 Agree

3 Neutral

2 Disagree

1 Strongly Disagree

1. Are task requirements clearly defined?
<--- Score

2. What sources do you use to gather information for a Automation Readiness study?
<--- Score

3. Who are the Automation Readiness improvement team members, including Management Leads and

Coaches?

<--- Score

4. Does the scope remain the same?

<--- Score

5. What system do you use for gathering Automation Readiness information?

<--- Score

6. How do you hand over Automation Readiness context?

<--- Score

7. If substitutes have been appointed, have they been briefed on the Automation Readiness goals and received regular communications as to the progress to date?

<--- Score

8. Are accountability and ownership for Automation Readiness clearly defined?

<--- Score

9. What are the record-keeping requirements of Automation Readiness activities?

<--- Score

10. What is the scope of the Automation Readiness effort?

<--- Score

11. Who approved the Automation Readiness scope?

<--- Score

12. What gets examined?

<--- Score

13. How do you gather the stories?

<--- Score

14. Has the Automation Readiness work been fairly and/or equitably divided and delegated among team members who are qualified and capable to perform the work? Has everyone contributed?

<--- Score

15. What baselines are required to be defined and managed?

<--- Score

16. What defines best in class?

<--- Score

17. How do you keep key subject matter experts in the loop?

<--- Score

18. How will variation in the actual durations of each activity be dealt with to ensure that the expected Automation Readiness results are met?

<--- Score

19. What is the worst case scenario?

<--- Score

20. Is the current 'as is' process being followed? If not, what are the discrepancies?

<--- Score

21. How would you define Automation Readiness

leadership?
<--- Score

22. Are the Automation Readiness requirements complete?
<--- Score

23. What knowledge or experience is required?
<--- Score

24. Are resources adequate for the scope?
<--- Score

25. Is there a critical path to deliver Automation Readiness results?
<--- Score

26. Do you all define Automation Readiness in the same way?
<--- Score

27. Is special Automation Readiness user knowledge required?
<--- Score

28. Who is gathering Automation Readiness information?
<--- Score

29. What are (control) requirements for Automation Readiness Information?
<--- Score

30. What are the requirements for audit information?
<--- Score

31. Have specific policy objectives been defined?
<--- Score

32. The political context: who holds power?
<--- Score

33. Does the team have regular meetings?
<--- Score

34. Has anyone else (internal or external to the group) attempted to solve this problem or a similar one before? If so, what knowledge can be leveraged from these previous efforts?
<--- Score

35. Are the Automation Readiness requirements testable?
<--- Score

36. What information should you gather?
<--- Score

37. What are the compelling stakeholder reasons for embarking on Automation Readiness?
<--- Score

38. What are the core elements of the Automation Readiness business case?
<--- Score

39. What specifically is the problem? Where does it occur? When does it occur? What is its extent?
<--- Score

40. What is the definition of Automation

Readiness excellence?
<--- Score

41. Is the work to date meeting requirements?
<--- Score

42. How do you catch Automation Readiness definition inconsistencies?
<--- Score

43. How do you manage changes in Automation Readiness requirements?
<--- Score

44. What is the definition of success?
<--- Score

45. Is the team adequately staffed with the desired cross-functionality? If not, what additional resources are available to the team?
<--- Score

46. How do you gather Automation Readiness requirements?
<--- Score

47. Do the problem and goal statements meet the SMART criteria (specific, measurable, attainable, relevant, and time-bound)?
<--- Score

48. How often are the team meetings?
<--- Score

49. How are consistent Automation Readiness definitions important?

<--- Score

50. Have the customer needs been translated into specific, measurable requirements? How?
<--- Score

51. In what way can you redefine the criteria of choice clients have in your category in your favor?
<--- Score

52. How does the Automation Readiness manager ensure against scope creep?
<--- Score

53. Are approval levels defined for contracts and supplements to contracts?
<--- Score

54. Has the direction changed at all during the course of Automation Readiness? If so, when did it change and why?
<--- Score

55. What Automation Readiness services do you require?
<--- Score

56. What are the Automation Readiness use cases?
<--- Score

57. How do you gather requirements?
<--- Score

58. Why are you doing Automation Readiness and what is the scope?
<--- Score

59. Is the scope of Automation Readiness defined?
<--- Score

60. What is out-of-scope initially?
<--- Score

61. Has your scope been defined?
<--- Score

62. Has/have the customer(s) been identified?
<--- Score

63. Is scope creep really all bad news?
<--- Score

64. How did the Automation Readiness manager receive input to the development of a Automation Readiness improvement plan and the estimated completion dates/times of each activity?
<--- Score

65. Has a project plan, Gantt chart, or similar been developed/completed?
<--- Score

66. When is/was the Automation Readiness start date?
<--- Score

67. Have all basic functions of Automation Readiness been defined?
<--- Score

68. What happens if Automation Readiness's scope changes?
<--- Score

69. What is the scope of Automation Readiness?
<--- Score

70. What intelligence can you gather?
<--- Score

71. When are meeting minutes sent out? Who is on the distribution list?
<--- Score

72. What is the scope of the Automation Readiness work?
<--- Score

73. Is Automation Readiness required?
<--- Score

74. Are there different segments of customers?
<--- Score

75. Is the improvement team aware of the different versions of a process: what they think it is vs. what it actually is vs. what it should be vs. what it could be?
<--- Score

76. Has a team charter been developed and communicated?
<--- Score

77. Has everyone on the team, including the team leaders, been properly trained?
<--- Score

78. What are the dynamics of the communication plan?

<--- Score

79. What are the Automation Readiness tasks and definitions?
<--- Score

80. How do you manage unclear Automation Readiness requirements?
<--- Score

81. How will the Automation Readiness team and the group measure complete success of Automation Readiness?
<--- Score

82. What is out of scope?
<--- Score

83. What is in scope?
<--- Score

84. Have all of the relationships been defined properly?
<--- Score

85. How do you manage scope?
<--- Score

86. Is there regularly 100% attendance at the team meetings? If not, have appointed substitutes attended to preserve cross-functionality and full representation?
<--- Score

87. What constraints exist that might impact the team?

<--- Score

88. Where can you gather more information?
<--- Score

89. What scope do you want your strategy to cover?
<--- Score

90. What are the Roles and Responsibilities for each team member and its leadership? Where is this documented?
<--- Score

91. Is Automation Readiness linked to key stakeholder goals and objectives?
<--- Score

92. Has the improvement team collected the 'voice of the customer' (obtained feedback – qualitative and quantitative)?
<--- Score

93. How do you think the partners involved in Automation Readiness would have defined success?
<--- Score

94. Will a Automation Readiness production readiness review be required?
<--- Score

95. How is the team tracking and documenting its work?
<--- Score

96. Is the Automation Readiness scope manageable?

<--- Score

97. Is there any additional Automation Readiness definition of success?
<--- Score

98. How have you defined all Automation Readiness requirements first?
<--- Score

99. What would be the goal or target for a Automation Readiness's improvement team?
<--- Score

100. Has a Automation Readiness requirement not been met?
<--- Score

101. Who defines (or who defined) the rules and roles?
<--- Score

102. How and when will the baselines be defined?
<--- Score

103. Do you have a Automation Readiness success story or case study ready to tell and share?
<--- Score

104. What key stakeholder process output measure(s) does Automation Readiness leverage and how?
<--- Score

105. How was the 'as is' process map developed, reviewed, verified and validated?
<--- Score

106. What critical content must be communicated –
who, what, when, where, and how?
<--- Score

107. Are there any constraints known that bear on the
ability to perform Automation Readiness work? How
is the team addressing them?
<--- Score

108. What information do you gather?
<--- Score

109. What is in the scope and what is not in scope?
<--- Score

110. Do you have organizational privacy
requirements?
<--- Score

111. What sort of initial information to gather?
<--- Score

112. Are roles and responsibilities formally defined?
<--- Score

113. Are different versions of process maps needed to
account for the different types of inputs?
<--- Score

114. What are the rough order estimates on cost
savings/opportunities that Automation Readiness
brings?
<--- Score

**115. Is it clearly defined in and to your
organization what you do?**

<--- Score

116. Are all requirements met?
<--- Score

117. Are required metrics defined, what are they?
<--- Score

118. What Automation Readiness requirements should be gathered?
<--- Score

119. How would you define the culture at your organization, how susceptible is it to Automation Readiness changes?
<--- Score

120. Has a high-level 'as is' process map been completed, verified and validated?
<--- Score

121. Is Automation Readiness currently on schedule according to the plan?
<--- Score

122. What are the boundaries of the scope? What is in bounds and what is not? What is the start point? What is the stop point?
<--- Score

123. What was the context?
<--- Score

124. When is the estimated completion date?
<--- Score

125. Who is gathering information?

<--- Score

126. Is the Automation Readiness scope complete and appropriately sized?

<--- Score

127. What is the context?

<--- Score

128. What customer feedback methods were used to solicit their input?

<--- Score

129. Is there a clear Automation Readiness case definition?

<--- Score

130. What is a worst-case scenario for losses?

<--- Score

Add up total points for this section:
_ _ _ _ _ = Total points for this section

Divided by: _ _ _ _ _ _ (number of statements answered) = _ _ _ _ _ _
Average score for this section

Transfer your score to the Automation Readiness Index at the beginning of the Self-Assessment.

CRITERION #3: MEASURE:

INTENT: Gather the correct data. Measure the current performance and evolution of the situation.

In my belief, the answer to this question is clearly defined:

5 Strongly Agree

4 Agree

3 Neutral

2 Disagree

1 Strongly Disagree

1. How can you measure the performance?
<--- Score

2. What details are required of the Automation Readiness cost structure?
<--- Score

3. What could cause delays in the schedule?
<--- Score

4. Have you made assumptions about the shape of the future, particularly its impact on your customers and competitors?

<--- Score

5. Has a cost center been established?

<--- Score

6. Which measures and indicators matter?

<--- Score

7. How will you measure your Automation Readiness effectiveness?

<--- Score

8. What does verifying compliance entail?

<--- Score

9. Have you included everything in your Automation Readiness cost models?

<--- Score

10. What does a Test Case verify?

<--- Score

11. What are the uncertainties surrounding estimates of impact?

<--- Score

12. Do you aggressively reward and promote the people who have the biggest impact on creating excellent Automation Readiness services/products?

<--- Score

13. What would it cost to replace your technology?

<--- Score

14. What are hidden Automation Readiness quality costs?
<--- Score

15. What measurements are being captured?
<--- Score

16. How do you aggregate measures across priorities?
<--- Score

17. How will you measure success?
<--- Score

18. What are the estimated costs of proposed changes?
<--- Score

19. What is your Automation Readiness quality cost segregation study?
<--- Score

20. What causes innovation to fail or succeed in your organization?
<--- Score

21. What are the types and number of measures to use?
<--- Score

22. Do the benefits outweigh the costs?
<--- Score

23. Do you effectively measure and reward individual

and team performance?
<--- Score

24. When a disaster occurs, who gets priority?
<--- Score

25. Is the solution cost-effective?
<--- Score

26. What is the total cost related to deploying
Automation Readiness, including any consulting or
professional services?
<--- Score

27. How do your measurements capture actionable
Automation Readiness information for use in
exceeding your customers expectations and securing
your customers engagement?
<--- Score

28. Are the units of measure consistent?
<--- Score

29. Are supply costs steady or fluctuating?
<--- Score

30. What are the costs?
<--- Score

31. Are actual costs in line with budgeted costs?
<--- Score

32. How will costs be allocated?
<--- Score

33. What are the costs of delaying Automation

Readiness action?

<--- Score

34. What does losing customers cost your organization?

<--- Score

35. What are you verifying?

<--- Score

36. What is the Automation Readiness business impact?

<--- Score

37. What do people want to verify?

<--- Score

38. Are the Automation Readiness benefits worth its costs?

<--- Score

39. How long to keep data and how to manage retention costs?

<--- Score

40. Does the Automation Readiness task fit the client's priorities?

<--- Score

41. How are costs allocated?

<--- Score

42. What is an unallowable cost?

<--- Score

43. When are costs are incurred?

<--- Score

44. Are the measurements objective?
<--- Score

45. What measurements are possible, practicable and meaningful?
<--- Score

46. How do you measure efficient delivery of Automation Readiness services?
<--- Score

47. What causes extra work or rework?
<--- Score

48. Did you tackle the cause or the symptom?
<--- Score

49. What drives O&M cost?
<--- Score

50. How can you manage cost down?
<--- Score

51. What relevant entities could be measured?
<--- Score

52. Do you have an issue in getting priority?
<--- Score

53. How do you verify and validate the Automation Readiness data?
<--- Score

54. What users will be impacted?

<--- Score

55. What are your operating costs?
<--- Score

56. Are you able to realize any cost savings?
<--- Score

57. What are the current costs of the Automation
Readiness process?
<--- Score

58. Which costs should be taken into account?
<--- Score

**59. How is the value delivered by Automation
Readiness being measured?**
<--- Score

60. What harm might be caused?
<--- Score

**61. How do you verify the authenticity of the data
and information used?**
<--- Score

62. Are there measurements based on task
performance?
<--- Score

63. What is your decision requirements diagram?
<--- Score

64. How much does it cost?
<--- Score

65. Will Automation Readiness have an impact on current business continuity, disaster recovery processes and/or infrastructure?

<--- Score

66. What is the total fixed cost?

<--- Score

67. What does your operating model cost?

<--- Score

68. How will success or failure be measured?

<--- Score

69. How is performance measured?

<--- Score

70. What do you measure and why?

<--- Score

71. What potential environmental factors impact the Automation Readiness effort?

<--- Score

72. Do you verify that corrective actions were taken?

<--- Score

73. How are measurements made?

<--- Score

74. How do you prevent mis-estimating cost?

<--- Score

75. Where can you go to verify the info?

<--- Score

76. What are the Automation Readiness key cost drivers?

<--- Score

77. What is the cause of any Automation Readiness gaps?

<--- Score

78. Where is it measured?

<--- Score

79. What happens if cost savings do not materialize?

<--- Score

80. When should you bother with diagrams?

<--- Score

81. Why do you expend time and effort to implement measurement, for whom?

<--- Score

82. How is progress measured?

<--- Score

83. How can you reduce costs?

<--- Score

84. How do you measure variability?

<--- Score

85. Is there an opportunity to verify requirements?

<--- Score

86. How do you verify Automation Readiness completeness and accuracy?

<--- Score

87. How do you verify the Automation Readiness requirements quality?

<--- Score

88. How do you verify your resources?

<--- Score

89. Who is involved in verifying compliance?

<--- Score

90. How sensitive must the Automation Readiness strategy be to cost?

<--- Score

91. How will effects be measured?

<--- Score

92. How do you measure success?

<--- Score

93. What is the cost of rework?

<--- Score

94. What is the root cause(s) of the problem?

<--- Score

95. How do you control the overall costs of your work processes?

<--- Score

96. How are you verifying it?

<--- Score

97. What disadvantage does this cause for the user?

<--- Score

98. What is measured? Why?
<--- Score

99. Why a Automation Readiness focus?
<--- Score

100. At what cost?
<--- Score

101. Was a business case (cost/benefit) developed?
<--- Score

102. Among the Automation Readiness product and service cost to be estimated, which is considered hardest to estimate?
<--- Score

103. What are your key Automation Readiness organizational performance measures, including key short and longer-term financial measures?
<--- Score

104. How do you verify if Automation Readiness is built right?
<--- Score

105. Is it possible to estimate the impact of unanticipated complexity such as wrong or failed assumptions, feedback, etcetera on proposed reforms?
<--- Score

106. What evidence is there and what is measured?
<--- Score

107. What are the operational costs after Automation Readiness deployment?

<--- Score

108. Are there competing Automation Readiness priorities?

<--- Score

109. Does management have the right priorities among projects?

<--- Score

110. How do you quantify and qualify impacts?

<--- Score

111. Does a Automation Readiness quantification method exist?

<--- Score

112. What are your primary costs, revenues, assets?

<--- Score

113. What would be a real cause for concern?

<--- Score

114. How can a Automation Readiness test verify your ideas or assumptions?

<--- Score

115. Which Automation Readiness impacts are significant?

<--- Score

116. What are the costs of reform?

<--- Score

117. How will your organization measure success?
<--- Score

118. Are indirect costs charged to the Automation Readiness program?
<--- Score

119. What can be used to verify compliance?
<--- Score

120. Do you have a flow diagram of what happens?
<--- Score

121. Are Automation Readiness vulnerabilities categorized and prioritized?
<--- Score

122. Are you taking your company in the direction of better and revenue or cheaper and cost?
<--- Score

123. Are you aware of what could cause a problem?
<--- Score

124. What are the costs and benefits?
<--- Score

125. Where is the cost?
<--- Score

126. Do you have any cost Automation Readiness limitation requirements?
<--- Score

127. What are your customers expectations and

measures?
<--- Score

128. Are missed Automation Readiness opportunities costing your organization money?
<--- Score

129. How will measures be used to manage and adapt?
<--- Score

130. How do you measure lifecycle phases?
<--- Score

131. How frequently do you track Automation Readiness measures?
<--- Score

132. What causes investor action?
<--- Score

133. What are the Automation Readiness investment costs?
<--- Score

134. Have design-to-cost goals been established?
<--- Score

135. Who pays the cost?
<--- Score

136. Is the cost worth the Automation Readiness effort ?
<--- Score

137. Are there any easy-to-implement alternatives to

Automation Readiness? Sometimes other solutions
are available that do not require the cost implications
of a full-blown project?
<--- Score

138. What methods are feasible and acceptable to
estimate the impact of reforms?
<--- Score

139. What could cause you to change course?
<--- Score

140. Why do the measurements/indicators matter?
<--- Score

Add up total points for this section:
_____ = Total points for this section

Divided by: _____ (number of
statements answered) = _____
Average score for this section

Transfer your score to the Automation
Readiness Index at the beginning of the
Self-Assessment.

CRITERION #4: ANALYZE:

INTENT: Analyze causes, assumptions and hypotheses.

In my belief, the answer to this question is clearly defined:

5 Strongly Agree

4 Agree

3 Neutral

2 Disagree

1 Strongly Disagree

1. How does the organization define, manage, and improve its Automation Readiness processes?
<--- Score

2. What are the Automation Readiness business drivers?
<--- Score

3. How do you identify specific Automation Readiness investment opportunities and emerging trends?

<--- Score

4. Were there any improvement opportunities identified from the process analysis?
<--- Score

5. How do you measure the operational performance of your key work systems and processes, including productivity, cycle time, and other appropriate measures of process effectiveness, efficiency, and innovation?
<--- Score

6. Who qualifies to gain access to data?
<--- Score

7. Do you, as a leader, bounce back quickly from setbacks?
<--- Score

8. Should you invest in industry-recognized qualifications?
<--- Score

9. What quality tools were used to get through the analyze phase?
<--- Score

10. What is the Value Stream Mapping?
<--- Score

11. What is your organizations system for selecting qualified vendors?
<--- Score

12. What conclusions were drawn from the team's

data collection and analysis? How did the team reach these conclusions?
<--- Score

13. What are your outputs?
<--- Score

14. What qualifications and skills do you need?
<--- Score

15. Do you have the authority to produce the output?
<--- Score

16. Who will gather what data?
<--- Score

17. Were Pareto charts (or similar) used to portray the 'heavy hitters' (or key sources of variation)?
<--- Score

18. What does the data say about the performance of the stakeholder process?
<--- Score

19. How will corresponding data be collected?
<--- Score

20. How often will data be collected for measures?
<--- Score

21. What output to create?
<--- Score

22. What are the processes for audit reporting and management?
<--- Score

23. Where is Automation Readiness data gathered?
<--- Score

24. Do you understand your management processes today?
<--- Score

25. Think about the functions involved in your Automation Readiness project, what processes flow from these functions?
<--- Score

26. Think about some of the processes you undertake within your organization, which do you own?
<--- Score

27. Which Automation Readiness data should be retained?
<--- Score

28. Record-keeping requirements flow from the records needed as inputs, outputs, controls and for transformation of a Automation Readiness process, are the records needed as inputs to the Automation Readiness process available?
<--- Score

29. What is the cost of poor quality as supported by the team's analysis?
<--- Score

30. What other jobs or tasks affect the performance of the steps in the Automation Readiness process?
<--- Score

31. Who owns what data?
<--- Score

32. Have you defined which data is gathered how?
<--- Score

33. Is there any way to speed up the process?
<--- Score

34. What are the best opportunities for value improvement?
<--- Score

35. Where can you get qualified talent today?
<--- Score

36. What are the revised rough estimates of the financial savings/opportunity for Automation Readiness improvements?
<--- Score

37. Is there an established change management process?
<--- Score

38. What controls do you have in place to protect data?
<--- Score

39. What, related to, Automation Readiness processes does your organization outsource?
<--- Score

40. Do your contracts/agreements contain data security obligations?

<--- Score

41. Who is involved in the management review process?
<--- Score

42. What process improvements will be needed?
<--- Score

43. An organizationally feasible system request is one that considers the mission, goals and objectives of the organization, key questions are: is the Automation Readiness solution request practical and will it solve a problem or take advantage of an opportunity to achieve company goals?
<--- Score

44. How much data can be collected in the given timeframe?
<--- Score

45. How do mission and objectives affect the Automation Readiness processes of your organization?
<--- Score

46. How is Automation Readiness data gathered?
<--- Score

47. What data is gathered?
<--- Score

48. Do your employees have the opportunity to do what they do best everyday?
<--- Score

49. What are your Automation Readiness processes?
<--- Score

50. How do you implement and manage your work processes to ensure that they meet design requirements?
<--- Score

51. Are all staff in core Automation Readiness subjects Highly Qualified?
<--- Score

52. Was a cause-and-effect diagram used to explore the different types of causes (or sources of variation)?
<--- Score

53. Do your leaders quickly bounce back from setbacks?
<--- Score

54. Is the Automation Readiness process severely broken such that a re-design is necessary?
<--- Score

55. Is the required Automation Readiness data gathered?
<--- Score

56. How will the Automation Readiness data be captured?
<--- Score

57. What is the output?
<--- Score

58. What other organizational variables, such as reward systems or communication systems, affect the performance of this Automation Readiness process?
<--- Score

59. How was the detailed process map generated, verified, and validated?
<--- Score

60. Do several people in different organizational units assist with the Automation Readiness process?
<--- Score

61. What qualifications are necessary?
<--- Score

62. What are your current levels and trends in key measures or indicators of Automation Readiness product and process performance that are important to and directly serve your customers? How do these results compare with the performance of your competitors and other organizations with similar offerings?
<--- Score

63. How do your work systems and key work processes relate to and capitalize on your core competencies?
<--- Score

64. How do you use Automation Readiness data and information to support organizational decision making and innovation?
<--- Score

65. What kind of crime could a potential new hire have committed that would not only not disqualify him/her from being hired by your organization, but would actually indicate that he/she might be a particularly good fit?
<--- Score

66. Identify an operational issue in your organization, for example, could a particular task be done more quickly or more efficiently by Automation Readiness?
<--- Score

67. What information qualified as important?
<--- Score

68. What were the financial benefits resulting from any 'ground fruit or low-hanging fruit' (quick fixes)?
<--- Score

69. Were any designed experiments used to generate additional insight into the data analysis?
<--- Score

70. Are your outputs consistent?
<--- Score

71. What Automation Readiness data should be managed?
<--- Score

72. Who will facilitate the team and process?
<--- Score

73. What are your key performance measures or indicators and in-process measures for the control

and improvement of your Automation Readiness processes?
<--- Score

74. What qualifications are needed?
<--- Score

75. Is the suppliers process defined and controlled?
<--- Score

76. What are the disruptive Automation Readiness technologies that enable your organization to radically change your business processes?
<--- Score

77. How are outputs preserved and protected?
<--- Score

78. What process should you select for improvement?
<--- Score

79. What tools were used to narrow the list of possible causes?
<--- Score

80. Did any value-added analysis or 'lean thinking' take place to identify some of the gaps shown on the 'as is' process map?
<--- Score

81. How do you define collaboration and team output?
<--- Score

82. Do staff qualifications match your project?
<--- Score

83. A compounding model resolution with available relevant data can often provide insight towards a solution methodology; which Automation Readiness models, tools and techniques are necessary?
<--- Score

84. Are gaps between current performance and the goal performance identified?
<--- Score

85. Is data and process analysis, root cause analysis and quantifying the gap/opportunity in place?
<--- Score

86. How do you promote understanding that opportunity for improvement is not criticism of the status quo, or the people who created the status quo?
<--- Score

87. What did the team gain from developing a sub-process map?
<--- Score

88. What is the oversight process?
<--- Score

89. What is the Automation Readiness Driver?
<--- Score

90. What methods do you use to gather Automation Readiness data?
<--- Score

91. Did any additional data need to be collected?
<--- Score

92. Have any additional benefits been identified that will result from closing all or most of the gaps?
<--- Score

93. What will drive Automation Readiness change?
<--- Score

94. What is your organizations process which leads to recognition of value generation?
<--- Score

95. Who gets your output?
<--- Score

96. Has an output goal been set?
<--- Score

97. How will the data be checked for quality?
<--- Score

98. What data do you need to collect?
<--- Score

99. Was a detailed process map created to amplify critical steps of the 'as is' stakeholder process?
<--- Score

100. What successful thing are you doing today that may be blinding you to new growth opportunities?
<--- Score

101. What qualifications do Automation Readiness leaders need?
<--- Score

102. What systems/processes must you excel at?
<--- Score

103. What internal processes need improvement?
<--- Score

104. What training and qualifications will you need?
<--- Score

105. Where is the data coming from to measure compliance?
<--- Score

106. How is the data gathered?
<--- Score

107. What qualifies as competition?
<--- Score

108. Have the problem and goal statements been updated to reflect the additional knowledge gained from the analyze phase?
<--- Score

109. What Automation Readiness data will be collected?
<--- Score

110. Has data output been validated?
<--- Score

111. How do you ensure that the Automation Readiness opportunity is realistic?
<--- Score

112. What Automation Readiness data do you gather

or use now?
<--- Score

113. Is the gap/opportunity displayed and communicated in financial terms?
<--- Score

114. Is the performance gap determined?
<--- Score

115. What Automation Readiness data should be collected?
<--- Score

116. Is pre-qualification of suppliers carried out?
<--- Score

117. How can risk management be tied procedurally to process elements?
<--- Score

118. How difficult is it to qualify what Automation Readiness ROI is?
<--- Score

119. How has the Automation Readiness data been gathered?
<--- Score

120. How is the Automation Readiness Value Stream Mapping managed?
<--- Score

121. What were the crucial 'moments of truth' on the process map?
<--- Score

122. What are your best practices for minimizing Automation Readiness project risk, while demonstrating incremental value and quick wins throughout the Automation Readiness project lifecycle?
<--- Score

123. Are Automation Readiness changes recognized early enough to be approved through the regular process?
<--- Score

124. What resources go in to get the desired output?
<--- Score

125. What are the necessary qualifications?
<--- Score

126. What are evaluation criteria for the output?
<--- Score

127. What are your current levels and trends in key Automation Readiness measures or indicators of product and process performance that are important to and directly serve your customers?
<--- Score

128. How is the way you as the leader think and process information affecting your organizational culture?
<--- Score

129. Do quality systems drive continuous improvement?
<--- Score

130. What types of data do your Automation Readiness indicators require?
<--- Score

131. What tools were used to generate the list of possible causes?
<--- Score

132. How will the change process be managed?
<--- Score

Add up total points for this section:
_ _ _ _ _ = Total points for this section

Divided by: _ _ _ _ _ _ (number of statements answered) = _ _ _ _ _ _
Average score for this section

Transfer your score to the Automation Readiness Index at the beginning of the Self-Assessment.

CRITERION #5: IMPROVE:

INTENT: Develop a practical solution. Innovate, establish and test the solution and to measure the results.

In my belief, the answer to this question is clearly defined:

5 Strongly Agree

4 Agree

3 Neutral

2 Disagree

1 Strongly Disagree

1. How can you better manage risk?
<--- Score

2. What Automation Readiness improvements can be made?
<--- Score

3. Is any Automation Readiness documentation required?

<--- Score

4. Which Automation Readiness solution is appropriate?
<--- Score

5. How are policy decisions made and where?
<--- Score

6. Who will be using the results of the measurement activities?
<--- Score

7. Have you achieved Automation Readiness improvements?
<--- Score

8. Is the solution technically practical?
<--- Score

9. Are the most efficient solutions problem-specific?
<--- Score

10. How does the team improve its work?
<--- Score

11. What are the Automation Readiness security risks?
<--- Score

12. Does a good decision guarantee a good outcome?
<--- Score

13. What is the team's contingency plan for potential problems occurring in implementation?
<--- Score

14. What were the underlying assumptions on the cost-benefit analysis?
<--- Score

15. What tools were most useful during the improve phase?
<--- Score

16. Do you have the optimal project management team structure?
<--- Score

17. How will you know when its improved?
<--- Score

18. How will you know that a change is an improvement?
<--- Score

19. To what extent does management recognize Automation Readiness as a tool to increase the results?
<--- Score

20. Is there a high likelihood that any recommendations will achieve their intended results?
<--- Score

21. Who are the Automation Readiness decision makers?
<--- Score

22. Are risk management tasks balanced centrally and locally?
<--- Score

23. How will you know that you have improved?
<--- Score

24. What improvements have been achieved?
<--- Score

25. Have you identified breakpoints and/or risk tolerances that will trigger broad consideration of a potential need for intervention or modification of strategy?
<--- Score

26. In the past few months, what is the smallest change you have made that has had the biggest positive result? What was it about that small change that produced the large return?
<--- Score

27. What tools do you use once you have decided on a Automation Readiness strategy and more importantly how do you choose?
<--- Score

28. Does the goal represent a desired result that can be measured?
<--- Score

29. Why improve in the first place?
<--- Score

30. How do you define the solutions' scope?
<--- Score

31. Which of the recognised risks out of all risks can be most likely transferred?

<--- Score

32. What is the Automation Readiness's sustainability risk?
<--- Score

33. Is risk periodically assessed?
<--- Score

34. Are decisions made in a timely manner?
<--- Score

35. Are risk triggers captured?
<--- Score

36. Was a pilot designed for the proposed solution(s)?
<--- Score

37. What needs improvement? Why?
<--- Score

38. Who makes the Automation Readiness decisions in your organization?
<--- Score

39. Are the key business and technology risks being managed?
<--- Score

40. Is the scope clearly documented?
<--- Score

41. What are the implications of the one critical Automation Readiness decision 10 minutes, 10 months, and 10 years from now?
<--- Score

42. Is Automation Readiness documentation maintained?
<--- Score

43. How scalable is your Automation Readiness solution?
<--- Score

44. What can you do to improve?
<--- Score

45. How do you measure progress and evaluate training effectiveness?
<--- Score

46. How is continuous improvement applied to risk management?
<--- Score

47. Is a solution implementation plan established, including schedule/work breakdown structure, resources, risk management plan, cost/budget, and control plan?
<--- Score

48. Is there a small-scale pilot for proposed improvement(s)? What conclusions were drawn from the outcomes of a pilot?
<--- Score

49. Are you assessing Automation Readiness and risk?
<--- Score

50. How do you measure risk?
<--- Score

51. Who manages supplier risk management in your organization?
<--- Score

52. At what point will vulnerability assessments be performed once Automation Readiness is put into production (e.g., ongoing Risk Management after implementation)?
<--- Score

53. How are Automation Readiness risks managed?
<--- Score

54. Who should make the Automation Readiness decisions?
<--- Score

55. How do you improve Automation Readiness service perception, and satisfaction?
<--- Score

56. Can the solution be designed and implemented within an acceptable time period?
<--- Score

57. What attendant changes will need to be made to ensure that the solution is successful?
<--- Score

58. Is the Automation Readiness solution sustainable?
<--- Score

59. Where do the Automation Readiness decisions reside?

<--- Score

60. How do you manage and improve your Automation Readiness work systems to deliver customer value and achieve organizational success and sustainability?
<--- Score

61. Who do you report Automation Readiness results to?
<--- Score

62. Can you integrate quality management and risk management?
<--- Score

63. How will you measure the results?
<--- Score

64. How do you decide how much to remunerate an employee?
<--- Score

65. What are your current levels and trends in key measures or indicators of workforce and leader development?
<--- Score

66. How do you go about comparing Automation Readiness approaches/solutions?
<--- Score

67. What is Automation Readiness's impact on utilizing the best solution(s)?
<--- Score

68. Risk events: what are the things that could go wrong?
<--- Score

69. How is knowledge sharing about risk management improved?
<--- Score

70. Is a contingency plan established?
<--- Score

71. How do you improve your likelihood of success ?
<--- Score

72. Who are the people involved in developing and implementing Automation Readiness?
<--- Score

73. Who will be responsible for making the decisions to include or exclude requested changes once Automation Readiness is underway?
<--- Score

74. Who are the key stakeholders for the Automation Readiness evaluation?
<--- Score

75. Who manages Automation Readiness risk?
<--- Score

76. How do you manage Automation Readiness risk?
<--- Score

77. Do those selected for the Automation Readiness team have a good general understanding of what Automation Readiness is

all about?
<--- Score

78. Is the optimal solution selected based on testing and analysis?
<--- Score

79. Where do you need Automation Readiness improvement?
<--- Score

80. How can skill-level changes improve Automation Readiness?
<--- Score

81. How do the Automation Readiness results compare with the performance of your competitors and other organizations with similar offerings?
<--- Score

82. Do vendor agreements bring new compliance risk ?
<--- Score

83. What is the risk?
<--- Score

84. How do you measure improved Automation Readiness service perception, and satisfaction?
<--- Score

85. What tools were used to evaluate the potential solutions?
<--- Score

86. Do you cover the five essential competencies:

Communication, Collaboration,Innovation, Adaptability, and Leadership that improve an organizations ability to leverage the new Automation Readiness in a volatile global economy?
<--- Score

87. Are procedures documented for managing Automation Readiness risks?
<--- Score

88. What risks do you need to manage?
<--- Score

89. What strategies for Automation Readiness improvement are successful?
<--- Score

90. Will the controls trigger any other risks?
<--- Score

91. What area needs the greatest improvement?
<--- Score

92. What are the affordable Automation Readiness risks?
<--- Score

93. What is the magnitude of the improvements?
<--- Score

94. Is the implementation plan designed?
<--- Score

95. Risk factors: what are the characteristics of Automation Readiness that make it risky?
<--- Score

96. How can you improve Automation Readiness?
<--- Score

97. What do you want to improve?
<--- Score

98. Is there a cost/benefit analysis of optimal solution(s)?
<--- Score

99. Do you combine technical expertise with business knowledge and Automation Readiness Key topics include lifecycles, development approaches, requirements and how to make a business case?
<--- Score

100. How do you deal with Automation Readiness risk?
<--- Score

101. How significant is the improvement in the eyes of the end user?
<--- Score

102. For decision problems, how do you develop a decision statement?
<--- Score

103. How does your organization evaluate strategic Automation Readiness success?
<--- Score

104. Explorations of the frontiers of Automation Readiness will help you build influence, improve Automation Readiness, optimize decision making,

and sustain change, what is your approach?
<--- Score

105. What tools were used to tap into the creativity and encourage 'outside the box' thinking?
<--- Score

106. What communications are necessary to support the implementation of the solution?
<--- Score

107. How risky is your organization?
<--- Score

108. Is supporting Automation Readiness documentation required?
<--- Score

109. Can you identify any significant risks or exposures to Automation Readiness third- parties (vendors, service providers, alliance partners etc) that concern you?
<--- Score

110. Is pilot data collected and analyzed?
<--- Score

111. How can the phases of Automation Readiness development be identified?
<--- Score

112. How do you link measurement and risk?
<--- Score

113. When you map the key players in your own work and the types/domains of relationships with

them, which relationships do you find easy and which challenging, and why?
<--- Score

114. What is the implementation plan?
<--- Score

115. What does the 'should be' process map/design look like?
<--- Score

116. What criteria will you use to assess your Automation Readiness risks?
<--- Score

117. If you could go back in time five years, what decision would you make differently? What is your best guess as to what decision you're making today you might regret five years from now?
<--- Score

118. Is the Automation Readiness risk managed?
<--- Score

119. Was a Automation Readiness charter developed?
<--- Score

120. Who will be responsible for documenting the Automation Readiness requirements in detail?
<--- Score

121. Were any criteria developed to assist the team in testing and evaluating potential solutions?
<--- Score

122. How risky is your organization?

<--- Score

**123. What practices helps your organization to
develop its capacity to recognize patterns?**
<--- Score

124. What actually has to improve and by how much?
<--- Score

125. What lessons, if any, from a pilot were
incorporated into the design of the full-scale solution?
<--- Score

126. Who controls key decisions that will be made?
<--- Score

127. What were the criteria for evaluating a
Automation Readiness pilot?
<--- Score

128. Would you develop a Automation Readiness
Communication Strategy?
<--- Score

129. What are the expected Automation Readiness
results?
<--- Score

130. What error proofing will be done to address some
of the discrepancies observed in the 'as is' process?
<--- Score

131. Are events managed to resolution?
<--- Score

132. Do you need to do a usability evaluation?

<--- Score

133. What should a proof of concept or pilot accomplish?
<--- Score

134. Is the measure of success for Automation Readiness understandable to a variety of people?
<--- Score

135. How do you improve productivity?
<--- Score

136. What is Automation Readiness risk?
<--- Score

137. What went well, what should change, what can improve?
<--- Score

138. Is the Automation Readiness documentation thorough?
<--- Score

Add up total points for this section:
_ _ _ _ _ = Total points for this section

Divided by: _ _ _ _ _ _ (number of statements answered) = _ _ _ _ _ _
Average score for this section

Transfer your score to the Automation Readiness Index at the beginning of the Self-Assessment.

CRITERION #6: CONTROL:

INTENT: Implement the practical solution. Maintain the performance and correct possible complications.

In my belief, the answer to this question is clearly defined:

5 Strongly Agree

4 Agree

3 Neutral

2 Disagree

1 Strongly Disagree

1. What should the next improvement project be that is related to Automation Readiness?
<--- Score

2. How will report readings be checked to effectively monitor performance?
<--- Score

3. How might the group capture best practices and

lessons learned so as to leverage improvements?
<--- Score

4. Who controls critical resources?
<--- Score

5. Do you monitor the Automation Readiness decisions made and fine tune them as they evolve?
<--- Score

6. What quality tools were useful in the control phase?
<--- Score

7. Are new process steps, standards, and documentation ingrained into normal operations?
<--- Score

8. Are pertinent alerts monitored, analyzed and distributed to appropriate personnel?
<--- Score

9. Against what alternative is success being measured?
<--- Score

10. What Automation Readiness standards are applicable?
<--- Score

11. You may have created your quality measures at a time when you lacked resources, technology wasn't up to the required standard, or low service levels were the industry norm. Have those circumstances changed?
<--- Score

12. Is reporting being used or needed?
<--- Score

13. How do you monitor usage and cost?
<--- Score

14. How will you measure your QA plan's effectiveness?
<--- Score

15. Will any special training be provided for results interpretation?
<--- Score

16. Do the viable solutions scale to future needs?
<--- Score

17. Will the team be available to assist members in planning investigations?
<--- Score

18. What key inputs and outputs are being measured on an ongoing basis?
<--- Score

19. What are the performance and scale of the Automation Readiness tools?
<--- Score

20. What is the best design framework for Automation Readiness organization now that, in a post industrial-age if the top-down, command and control model is no longer relevant?
<--- Score

21. Are controls in place and consistently applied?

<--- Score

22. Is a response plan in place for when the input, process, or output measures indicate an 'out-of-control' condition?
<--- Score

23. How do you encourage people to take control and responsibility?
<--- Score

24. Is there a standardized process?
<--- Score

25. Is knowledge gained on process shared and institutionalized?
<--- Score

26. How is change control managed?
<--- Score

27. Are suggested corrective/restorative actions indicated on the response plan for known causes to problems that might surface?
<--- Score

28. Do the Automation Readiness decisions you make today help people and the planet tomorrow?
<--- Score

29. Who has control over resources?
<--- Score

30. Does the response plan contain a definite closed loop continual improvement scheme (e.g., plan-do-check-act)?

<--- Score

31. How do controls support value?
<--- Score

32. How will new or emerging customer needs/
requirements be checked/communicated to orient
the process toward meeting the new specifications
and continually reducing variation?
<--- Score

33. What can you control?
<--- Score

34. How will Automation Readiness decisions be
made and monitored?
<--- Score

35. What other areas of the group might benefit from
the Automation Readiness team's improvements,
knowledge, and learning?
<--- Score

36. What do you measure to verify effectiveness
gains?
<--- Score

37. How do you establish and deploy modified action
plans if circumstances require a shift in plans and
rapid execution of new plans?
<--- Score

38. What are the key elements of your Automation
Readiness performance improvement system,
including your evaluation, organizational learning,
and innovation processes?

<--- Score

39. Does job training on the documented procedures need to be part of the process team's education and training?
<--- Score

40. How will the process owner verify improvement in present and future sigma levels, process capabilities?
<--- Score

41. Is there a transfer of ownership and knowledge to process owner and process team tasked with the responsibilities.
<--- Score

42. What is your plan to assess your security risks?
<--- Score

43. How is Automation Readiness project cost planned, managed, monitored?
<--- Score

44. In the case of a Automation Readiness project, the criteria for the audit derive from implementation objectives, an audit of a Automation Readiness project involves assessing whether the recommendations outlined for implementation have been met, can you track that any Automation Readiness project is implemented as planned, and is it working?
<--- Score

45. Have new or revised work instructions resulted?
<--- Score

46. Is there an action plan in case of emergencies?
<--- Score

47. Can support from partners be adjusted?
<--- Score

48. What do you stand for--and what are you against?
<--- Score

49. Is new knowledge gained imbedded in the response plan?
<--- Score

50. What is the recommended frequency of auditing?
<--- Score

51. What are customers monitoring?
<--- Score

52. Can you adapt and adjust to changing Automation Readiness situations?
<--- Score

53. How do your controls stack up?
<--- Score

54. What is the control/monitoring plan?
<--- Score

55. How will the process owner and team be able to hold the gains?
<--- Score

56. Are there documented procedures?
<--- Score

57. Is there documentation that will support the successful operation of the improvement?
<--- Score

58. How do you select, collect, align, and integrate Automation Readiness data and information for tracking daily operations and overall organizational performance, including progress relative to strategic objectives and action plans?
<--- Score

59. Does the Automation Readiness performance meet the customer's requirements?
<--- Score

60. Do you monitor the effectiveness of your Automation Readiness activities?
<--- Score

61. Has the Automation Readiness value of standards been quantified?
<--- Score

62. Does Automation Readiness appropriately measure and monitor risk?
<--- Score

63. What are you attempting to measure/monitor?
<--- Score

64. What are the critical parameters to watch?
<--- Score

65. Who sets the Automation Readiness standards?
<--- Score

66. What is your theory of human motivation, and how does your compensation plan fit with that view?

<--- Score

67. Is there a Automation Readiness Communication plan covering who needs to get what information when?

<--- Score

68. Implementation Planning: is a pilot needed to test the changes before a full roll out occurs?

<--- Score

69. Are the Automation Readiness standards challenging?

<--- Score

70. Is there a documented and implemented monitoring plan?

<--- Score

71. What is the standard for acceptable Automation Readiness performance?

<--- Score

72. Act/Adjust: What Do you Need to Do Differently?

<--- Score

73. How will input, process, and output variables be checked to detect for sub-optimal conditions?

<--- Score

74. Are the planned controls in place?

<--- Score

75. Are documented procedures clear and easy to follow for the operators?
<--- Score

76. How likely is the current Automation Readiness plan to come in on schedule or on budget?
<--- Score

77. How will the day-to-day responsibilities for monitoring and continual improvement be transferred from the improvement team to the process owner?
<--- Score

78. Who is going to spread your message?
<--- Score

79. Does a troubleshooting guide exist or is it needed?
<--- Score

80. Is a response plan established and deployed?
<--- Score

81. How do you plan for the cost of succession?
<--- Score

82. Will your goals reflect your program budget?
<--- Score

83. Are operating procedures consistent?
<--- Score

84. Is there a recommended audit plan for routine surveillance inspections of Automation Readiness's

gains?

<--- Score

85. How can you best use all of your knowledge repositories to enhance learning and sharing?

<--- Score

86. Who is the Automation Readiness process owner?

<--- Score

87. What adjustments to the strategies are needed?

<--- Score

88. What do your reports reflect?

<--- Score

89. Is there a control plan in place for sustaining improvements (short and long-term)?

<--- Score

90. Where do ideas that reach policy makers and planners as proposals for Automation Readiness strengthening and reform actually originate?

<--- Score

91. How do senior leaders actions reflect a commitment to the organizations Automation Readiness values?

<--- Score

92. How do you spread information?

<--- Score

93. What are the known security controls?

<--- Score

94. How widespread is its use?
<--- Score

95. Has the improved process and its steps been standardized?
<--- Score

96. What are your results for key measures or indicators of the accomplishment of your Automation Readiness strategy and action plans, including building and strengthening core competencies?
<--- Score

97. Who will be in control?
<--- Score

98. What should you measure to verify efficiency gains?
<--- Score

99. What other systems, operations, processes, and infrastructures (hiring practices, staffing, training, incentives/rewards, metrics/dashboards/scorecards, etc.) need updates, additions, changes, or deletions in order to facilitate knowledge transfer and improvements?
<--- Score

Add up total points for this section:
_ _ _ _ _ = Total points for this section

Divided by: _ _ _ _ _ _ (number of statements answered) = _ _ _ _ _ _
Average score for this section

Transfer your score to the Automation
Readiness Index at the beginning of the
Self-Assessment.

CRITERION #7: SUSTAIN:

INTENT: Retain the benefits.

In my belief, the answer to this question is clearly defined:

5 Strongly Agree

4 Agree

3 Neutral

2 Disagree

1 Strongly Disagree

1. How do you listen to customers to obtain actionable information?
<--- Score

2. Why do and why don't your customers like your organization?
<--- Score

3. To whom do you add value?
<--- Score

4. How do you keep the momentum going?
<--- Score

5. Are the criteria for selecting recommendations stated?
<--- Score

6. What current systems have to be understood and/or changed?
<--- Score

7. Is it economical; do you have the time and money?
<--- Score

8. Are you / should you be revolutionary or evolutionary?
<--- Score

9. Will it be accepted by users?
<--- Score

10. Who is responsible for errors?
<--- Score

11. Who is on the team?
<--- Score

12. What are the potential basics of Automation Readiness fraud?
<--- Score

13. Who uses your product in ways you never expected?
<--- Score

14. If your customer were your grandmother,

would you tell her to buy what you're selling?
<--- Score

15. What is your Automation Readiness strategy?
<--- Score

16. How are you doing compared to your industry?
<--- Score

17. What stupid rule would you most like to kill?
<--- Score

18. What is an unauthorized commitment?
<--- Score

19. What could happen if you do not do it?
<--- Score

20. At what moment would you think; Will I get fired?
<--- Score

21. How do you create buy-in?
<--- Score

22. What is your formula for success in Automation Readiness ?
<--- Score

23. Is there any existing Automation Readiness governance structure?
<--- Score

24. What is the range of capabilities?
<--- Score

25. If you got fired and a new hire took your place,

what would she do different?

<--- Score

26. Operational - will it work?

<--- Score

27. What is the purpose of Automation Readiness in relation to the mission?

<--- Score

28. What will be the consequences to the stakeholder (financial, reputation etc) if Automation Readiness does not go ahead or fails to deliver the objectives?

<--- Score

29. Do you have past Automation Readiness successes?

<--- Score

30. Are all key stakeholders present at all Structured Walkthroughs?

<--- Score

31. What is your question? Why?

<--- Score

32. Is Automation Readiness realistic, or are you setting yourself up for failure?

<--- Score

33. How do you proactively clarify deliverables and Automation Readiness quality expectations?

<--- Score

34. How do you know if you are successful?

<--- Score

35. What goals did you miss?

<--- Score

36. What is the overall business strategy?

<--- Score

37. What happens if you do not have enough funding?

<--- Score

38. What is it like to work for you?

<--- Score

39. Who, on the executive team or the board, has spoken to a customer recently?

<--- Score

40. What are the key enablers to make this Automation Readiness move?

<--- Score

41. How will you motivate the stakeholders with the least vested interest?

<--- Score

42. What is the kind of project structure that would be appropriate for your Automation Readiness project, should it be formal and complex, or can it be less formal and relatively simple?

<--- Score

43. What you are going to do to affect the numbers?

<--- Score

44. Who are your customers?

<--- Score

45. Which models, tools and techniques are necessary?
<--- Score

46. What are your personal philosophies regarding Automation Readiness and how do they influence your work?
<--- Score

47. If you do not follow, then how to lead?
<--- Score

48. Do you have the right people on the bus?
<--- Score

49. Who will determine interim and final deadlines?
<--- Score

50. Marketing budgets are tighter, consumers are more skeptical, and social media has changed forever the way we talk about Automation Readiness, how do you gain traction?
<--- Score

51. Who will be responsible for deciding whether Automation Readiness goes ahead or not after the initial investigations?
<--- Score

52. Who are the key stakeholders?
<--- Score

53. Do you have the right capabilities and capacities?
<--- Score

54. What are current Automation Readiness paradigms?

<--- Score

55. What are internal and external Automation Readiness relations?

<--- Score

56. How do you ensure that implementations of Automation Readiness products are done in a way that ensures safety?

<--- Score

57. What Automation Readiness modifications can you make work for you?

<--- Score

58. Do you know who is a friend or a foe?

<--- Score

59. How do you govern and fulfill your societal responsibilities?

<--- Score

60. Can you maintain your growth without detracting from the factors that have contributed to your success?

<--- Score

61. Why is it important to have senior management support for a Automation Readiness project?

<--- Score

62. What is the source of the strategies for Automation

Readiness strengthening and reform?
<--- Score

63. When information truly is ubiquitous, when reach and connectivity are completely global, when computing resources are infinite, and when a whole new set of impossibilities are not only possible, but happening, what will that do to your business?
<--- Score

64. Which Automation Readiness goals are the most important?
<--- Score

65. If you weren't already in this business, would you enter it today? And if not, what are you going to do about it?
<--- Score

66. What management system can you use to leverage the Automation Readiness experience, ideas, and concerns of the people closest to the work to be done?
<--- Score

67. How important is Automation Readiness to the user organizations mission?
<--- Score

68. Where can you break convention?
<--- Score

69. Are you changing as fast as the world around you?
<--- Score

70. How do you manage Automation Readiness Knowledge Management (KM)?

<--- Score

71. How can you negotiate Automation Readiness successfully with a stubborn boss, an irate client, or a deceitful coworker?

<--- Score

72. What is the estimated value of the project?

<--- Score

73. If you had to rebuild your organization without any traditional competitive advantages (i.e., no killer technology, promising research, innovative product/service delivery model, etcetera), how would your people have to approach their work and collaborate together in order to create the necessary conditions for success?

<--- Score

74. What would you recommend your friend do if he/she were facing this dilemma?

<--- Score

75. Whose voice (department, ethnic group, women, older workers, etc) might you have missed hearing from in your company, and how might you amplify this voice to create positive momentum for your business?

<--- Score

76. Do you say no to customers for no reason?

<--- Score

77. What is the overall talent health of your organization as a whole at senior levels, and for each organization reporting to a member of the Senior Leadership Team?

<--- Score

78. What Automation Readiness skills are most important?

<--- Score

79. What must you excel at?

<--- Score

80. How do you foster the skills, knowledge, talents, attributes, and characteristics you want to have?

<--- Score

81. What may be the consequences for the performance of an organization if all stakeholders are not consulted regarding Automation Readiness?

<--- Score

82. How will you insure seamless interoperability of Automation Readiness moving forward?

<--- Score

83. Who do we want your customers to become?

<--- Score

84. What would have to be true for the option on the table to be the best possible choice?

<--- Score

85. Is a Automation Readiness team work effort in place?

<--- Score

86. What happens when a new employee joins the organization?

<--- Score

87. What does your signature ensure?

<--- Score

88. What have been your experiences in defining long range Automation Readiness goals?

<--- Score

89. What is your competitive advantage?

<--- Score

90. What are the business goals Automation Readiness is aiming to achieve?

<--- Score

91. Can the schedule be done in the given time?

<--- Score

92. How do you keep records, of what?

<--- Score

93. What knowledge, skills and characteristics mark a good Automation Readiness project manager?

<--- Score

94. How is implementation research currently incorporated into each of your goals?

<--- Score

95. How do senior leaders deploy your organizations vision and values through your leadership system, to the workforce, to key

suppliers and partners, and to customers and other stakeholders, as appropriate?
<--- Score

96. Do you think Automation Readiness accomplishes the goals you expect it to accomplish?
<--- Score

97. Who is responsible for ensuring appropriate resources (time, people and money) are allocated to Automation Readiness?
<--- Score

98. Is maximizing Automation Readiness protection the same as minimizing Automation Readiness loss?
<--- Score

99. How do you engage the workforce, in addition to satisfying them?
<--- Score

100. How likely is it that a customer would recommend your company to a friend or colleague?
<--- Score

101. What unique value proposition (UVP) do you offer?
<--- Score

102. What have you done to protect your business from competitive encroachment?
<--- Score

103. What information is critical to your organization that your executives are ignoring?

<--- Score

104. What is the funding source for this project?
<--- Score

105. Who have you, as a company, historically been when you've been at your best?
<--- Score

106. What is a feasible sequencing of reform initiatives over time?
<--- Score

107. If no one would ever find out about your accomplishments, how would you lead differently?
<--- Score

108. How do you foster innovation?
<--- Score

109. What are the challenges?
<--- Score

110. Are you using a design thinking approach and integrating Innovation, Automation Readiness Experience, and Brand Value?
<--- Score

111. Who is the main stakeholder, with ultimate responsibility for driving Automation Readiness forward?
<--- Score

112. Political -is anyone trying to undermine this project?
<--- Score

113. What one word do you want to own in the minds of your customers, employees, and partners?
<--- Score

114. Do you have an implicit bias for capital investments over people investments?
<--- Score

115. Do you feel that more should be done in the Automation Readiness area?
<--- Score

116. Who do you think the world wants your organization to be?
<--- Score

117. What are the success criteria that will indicate that Automation Readiness objectives have been met and the benefits delivered?
<--- Score

118. What are strategies for increasing support and reducing opposition?
<--- Score

119. What new services of functionality will be implemented next with Automation Readiness ?
<--- Score

120. Think of your Automation Readiness project, what are the main functions?
<--- Score

121. What should you stop doing?

<--- Score

122. Ask yourself: how would you do this work if you only had one staff member to do it?
<--- Score

123. How do you provide a safe environment -physically and emotionally?
<--- Score

124. Who do you want your customers to become?
<--- Score

125. How do you track customer value, profitability or financial return, organizational success, and sustainability?
<--- Score

126. What trophy do you want on your mantle?
<--- Score

127. Are the assumptions believable and achievable?
<--- Score

128. What is something you believe that nearly no one agrees with you on?
<--- Score

129. Why should people listen to you?
<--- Score

130. What are the barriers to increased Automation Readiness production?
<--- Score

131. If you find that you havent accomplished one

of the goals for one of the steps of the Automation Readiness strategy, what will you do to fix it?
<--- Score

132. What are the short and long-term Automation Readiness goals?
<--- Score

133. In a project to restructure Automation Readiness outcomes, which stakeholders would you involve?
<--- Score

134. Is there a work around that you can use?
<--- Score

135. What happens at your organization when people fail?
<--- Score

136. What did you miss in the interview for the worst hire you ever made?
<--- Score

137. Whom among your colleagues do you trust, and for what?
<--- Score

138. Why will customers want to buy your organizations products/services?
<--- Score

139. Who are four people whose careers you have enhanced?
<--- Score

140. Is your basic point _____ or _____?

<--- Score

141. How do you make it meaningful in connecting Automation Readiness with what users do day-to-day?

<--- Score

142. Is Automation Readiness dependent on the successful delivery of a current project?

<--- Score

143. Which individuals, teams or departments will be involved in Automation Readiness?

<--- Score

144. How long will it take to change?

<--- Score

145. Do you think you know, or do you know you know ?

<--- Score

146. Which functions and people interact with the supplier and or customer?

<--- Score

147. How do you accomplish your long range Automation Readiness goals?

<--- Score

148. How do you determine the key elements that affect Automation Readiness workforce satisfaction, how are these elements determined for different workforce groups and segments?

<--- Score

149. Are assumptions made in Automation Readiness stated explicitly?

<--- Score

150. How do you transition from the baseline to the target?

<--- Score

151. What are the long-term Automation Readiness goals?

<--- Score

152. What are your most important goals for the strategic Automation Readiness objectives?

<--- Score

153. What projects are going on in the organization today, and what resources are those projects using from the resource pools?

<--- Score

154. What are you trying to prove to yourself, and how might it be hijacking your life and business success?

<--- Score

155. What was the last experiment you ran?

<--- Score

156. Is the Automation Readiness organization completing tasks effectively and efficiently?

<--- Score

157. What is your BATNA (best alternative to a negotiated agreement)?

<--- Score

158. Would you rather sell to knowledgeable and informed customers or to uninformed customers?
<--- Score

159. What potential megatrends could make your business model obsolete?
<--- Score

160. Are you making progress, and are you making progress as Automation Readiness leaders?
<--- Score

161. How will you know that the Automation Readiness project has been successful?
<--- Score

162. What are you challenging?
<--- Score

163. How do you set Automation Readiness stretch targets and how do you get people to not only participate in setting these stretch targets but also that they strive to achieve these?
<--- Score

164. What is the recommended frequency of auditing?
<--- Score

165. What role does communication play in the success or failure of a Automation Readiness project?
<--- Score

166. What are the top 3 things at the forefront of your Automation Readiness agendas for the next 3

years?
<--- Score

167. Who else should you help?
<--- Score

168. Can you do all this work?
<--- Score

169. Are you maintaining a past–present–future perspective throughout the Automation Readiness discussion?
<--- Score

170. Who will provide the final approval of Automation Readiness deliverables?
<--- Score

Add up total points for this section:
_ _ _ _ _ = Total points for this section

Divided by: _ _ _ _ _ _ (number of statements answered) = _ _ _ _ _ _
Average score for this section

Transfer your score to the Automation Readiness Index at the beginning of the Self-Assessment.

Automation Readiness and Managing Projects, Criteria for Project Managers:

1.0 Initiating Process Group: Automation Readiness

1. In which Automation Readiness project management process group is the detailed Automation Readiness project budget created?

2. Do you understand all business (operational), technical, resource and vendor risks associated with the Automation Readiness project?

3. Who is behind the Automation Readiness project?

4. When will the Automation Readiness project be done?

5. How will it affect me?

6. What will you do?

7. What will you do to minimize the impact should a risk event occur?

8. Do you know all the stakeholders impacted by the Automation Readiness project and what needs are?

9. Did the Automation Readiness project team have the right skills?

10. When must it be done?

11. For technology Automation Readiness projects only: Are all production support stakeholders (Business unit, technical support, & user) prepared for implementation with appropriate contingency plans?

12. What communication items need improvement?

13. How can you make your needs known?

14. Does the Automation Readiness project team have enough people to execute the Automation Readiness project plan?

15. How will you do it?

16. Where must it be done?

17. At which cmmi level are software processes documented, standardized, and integrated into a standard to-be practiced process for your organization?

18. The process to Manage Stakeholders is part of which process group?

19. How to control and approve each phase?

20. Were resources available as planned?

1.1 Project Charter: Automation Readiness

21. Is it an improvement over existing products?

22. How will you learn more about the process or system you are trying to improve?

23. When will this occur?

24. Is time of the essence?

25. What outcome, in measureable terms, are you hoping to accomplish?

26. If finished, on what date did it finish?

27. What goes into your Automation Readiness project Charter?

28. When?

29. Strategic fit: what is the strategic initiative identifier for this Automation Readiness project?

30. Dependent Automation Readiness projects: what Automation Readiness projects must be underway or completed before this Automation Readiness project can be successful?

31. Why the improvements?

32. Why have you chosen the aim you have set forth?

33. Automation Readiness project objective statement: what must the Automation Readiness project do?

34. Why use a Automation Readiness project charter?

35. Why executive support?

36. What are some examples of a business case?

37. Who is the Automation Readiness project Manager?

38. What does it need to do?

39. Avoid costs, improve service, and/ or comply with a mandate?

1.2 Stakeholder Register: Automation Readiness

40. Who are the stakeholders?

41. How big is the gap?

42. What is the power of the stakeholder?

43. How should employers make voices heard?

44. Who wants to talk about Security?

45. Is your organization ready for change?

46. How will reports be created?

47. What & Why?

48. Who is managing stakeholder engagement?

49. How much influence do they have on the Automation Readiness project?

50. What are the major Automation Readiness project milestones requiring communications or providing communications opportunities?

51. What opportunities exist to provide communications?

1.3 Stakeholder Analysis Matrix: Automation Readiness

52. What are the reimbursement requirements?

53. Could any of your organizations weaknesses seriously threaten development?

54. Disadvantages of proposition?

55. Economy - home, abroad?

56. Who holds positions of responsibility in interested organizations?

57. Usps (unique selling points)?

58. New technologies, services, ideas?

59. Are the interests in line with the program objectives?

60. What tools would help you communicate?

61. Political effects?

62. What can the stakeholder prevent from happening?

63. Who determines value?

64. Who will be affected by the Automation Readiness project?

65. What is the stakeholders name, what is function?

66. Who will be affected by the work?

67. What do people from other organizations see as your strengths?

68. What mechanisms are proposed to monitor and measure Automation Readiness project performance in terms of social development outcomes?

69. Identify the stakeholders levels most frequently used –or at least sought– in your Automation Readiness projects and for which purpose?

70. How can you counter negative efforts?

2.0 Planning Process Group: Automation Readiness

71. In what way has the Automation Readiness project come up with innovative measures for problem-solving?

72. How well did the chosen processes fit the needs of the Automation Readiness project?

73. What good practices or successful experiences or transferable examples have been identified?

74. How are it Automation Readiness projects different?

75. Professionals want to know what is expected from them; what are the deliverables?

76. To what extent have public/private national resources and/or counterparts been mobilized to contribute to the programs objective and produce results and impacts?

77. Is the identification of the problems, inequalities and gaps, with respective causes, clear in the Automation Readiness project?

78. In which Automation Readiness project management process group is the detailed Automation Readiness project budget created?

79. What factors are contributing to progress or delay

in the achievement of products and results?

80. Why do it Automation Readiness projects fail?

81. What should you do next?

82. Are the follow-up indicators relevant and do they meet the quality needed to measure the outputs and outcomes of the Automation Readiness project?

83. Does the program have follow-up mechanisms (to verify the quality of the products, punctuality of delivery, etc.) to measure progress in the achievement of the envisaged results?

84. What are the different approaches to building the WBS?

85. To what extent are the participating departments coordinating with each other?

86. How well do the team follow the chosen processes?

87. Are you just doing busywork to pass the time?

88. Is the Automation Readiness project supported by national and/or local organizations?

89. How well defined and documented are the Automation Readiness project management processes you chose to use?

90. In what ways can the governance of the Automation Readiness project be improved so that it has greater likelihood of achieving future

sustainability?

2.1 Project Management Plan: Automation Readiness

91. How do you manage integration?

92. What are the assigned resources?

93. How well are you able to manage your risk?

94. Are there any Client staffing expectations?

95. Is there an incremental analysis/cost effectiveness analysis of proposed mitigation features based on an approved method and using an accepted model?

96. Are the proposed Automation Readiness project purposes different than a previously authorized Automation Readiness project?

97. Who is the Automation Readiness project Manager?

98. Are there non-structural buyout or relocation recommendations?

99. Do there need to be organizational changes?

100. Where does all this information come from?

101. When is the Automation Readiness project management plan created?

102. What are the deliverables?

103. What if, for example, the positive direction and vision of your organization causes expected trends to change resulting in greater need than expected?

104. What would you do differently?

105. If the Automation Readiness project is complex or scope is specialized, do you have appropriate and/or qualified staff available to perform the tasks?

106. What is risk management?

107. What would you do differently what did not work?

108. Has the selected plan been formulated using cost effectiveness and incremental analysis techniques?

2.2 Scope Management Plan: Automation Readiness

109. Are vendor invoices audited for accuracy before payment?

110. Sensitivity analysis?

111. Will your organizations estimating methodology be used and followed?

112. What are the risks of not having good inter-organization cooperation on the Automation Readiness project?

113. What is the unique product, service or result?

114. Are enough systems & user personnel assigned to the Automation Readiness project?

115. What if you do not have more detailed information on the report?

116. Alignment to strategic goals & objectives?

117. What does the critical path really mean?

118. Quality standards - are controls in place to ensure that the work was not only completed and also completed to meet specific standards?

119. Are meeting minutes captured and sent out after the meeting?

120. Do you have the reasons why the changes to your organizational systems and capabilities are required?

121. Are any non-compliance issues that exist due to organizations practices?

122. Is the schedule updated on a periodic basis?

123. Have the key elements of a coherent Automation Readiness project management strategy been established?

124. Have all documents been archived in a Automation Readiness project repository for each release?

125. How difficult will it be to do specific activities on this Automation Readiness project?

126. What should you drop in order to add something new?

127. Has the scope management document been updated and distributed to help prevent scope creep?

128. Where do scope processes fit in?

2.3 Requirements Management Plan: Automation Readiness

129. Is the user satisfied?

130. What information regarding the Automation Readiness project requirements will be reported?

131. Will you document changes to requirements?

132. Have stakeholders been instructed in the Change Control process?

133. How detailed should the Automation Readiness project get?

134. If it exists, where is it housed?

135. Did you avoid subjective, flowery or non-specific statements?

136. Does the Automation Readiness project have a Change Control process?

137. What are you counting on?

138. What are you trying to do?

139. How will the information be distributed?

140. Controlling Automation Readiness project requirements involves monitoring the status of the Automation Readiness project requirements

and managing changes to the requirements. Who is responsible for monitoring and tracking the Automation Readiness project requirements?

141. Who will perform the analysis?

142. How often will the reporting occur?

143. Do you have an appropriate arrangement for meetings?

144. Is stakeholder risk tolerance an important factor for the requirements process in this Automation Readiness project?

145. What cost metrics will be used?

146. Will the product release be stable and mature enough to be deployed in the user community?

147. Is infrastructure setup part of your Automation Readiness project?

148. Who will do the reporting and to whom will reports be delivered?

2.4 Requirements Documentation: Automation Readiness

149. Are all functions required by the customer included?

150. How does the proposed Automation Readiness project contribute to the overall objectives of your organization?

151. How do you know when a Requirement is accurate enough?

152. What will be the integration problems?

153. What are the acceptance criteria?

154. What are the potential disadvantages/ advantages?

155. Consistency. are there any requirements conflicts?

156. Where are business rules being captured?

157. How will requirements be documented and who signs off on them?

158. What kind of entity is a problem ?

159. How will they be documented / shared?

160. What marketing channels do you want to use:

e-mail, letter or sms?

161. Does your organization restrict technical alternatives?

162. What are the attributes of a customer?

163. What is the risk associated with cost and schedule?

164. Who is involved?

165. How does what is being described meet the business need?

166. What images does it conjure?

167. Who is interacting with the system?

168. What if the system wasn t implemented?

2.5 Requirements Traceability Matrix: Automation Readiness

169. How will it affect the stakeholders personally in career?

170. What percentage of Automation Readiness projects are producing traceability matrices between requirements and other work products?

171. What is the WBS?

172. Do you have a clear understanding of all subcontracts in place?

173. Is there a requirements traceability process in place?

174. Why use a WBS?

175. How small is small enough?

176. Why do you manage scope?

177. Will you use a Requirements Traceability Matrix?

178. What are the chronologies, contingencies, consequences, criteria?

179. How do you manage scope?

180. Describe the process for approving requirements so they can be added to the traceability matrix

and Automation Readiness project work can be performed. Will the Automation Readiness project requirements become approved in writing?

2.6 Project Scope Statement: Automation Readiness

181. Have the configuration management functions been assigned?

182. Is the plan for your organization of the Automation Readiness project resources adequate?

183. Once its defined, what is the stability of the Automation Readiness project scope?

184. Is there a Quality Assurance Plan documented and filed?

185. Elements of scope management that deal with concept development ?

186. Automation Readiness project lead, team lead, solution architect?

187. Is the quality function identified and assigned?

188. Will the risk status be reported to management on a regular and frequent basis?

189. Who will you recommend approve the change, and when do you recommend the change reviews occur?

190. Are the meetings set up to have assigned note takers that will add action/issues to the issue list?

191. If there is an independent oversight contractor, have they signed off on the Automation Readiness project Plan?

192. How often do you estimate that the scope might change, and why?

193. Will there be a Change Control Process in place?

194. What are the major deliverables of the Automation Readiness project?

195. If the scope changes, what will the impact be to your Automation Readiness project in terms of duration, cost, quality, or any other important areas of the Automation Readiness project?

196. Have the reports to be produced, distributed, and filed been defined?

197. If you were to write a list of what should not be included in the scope statement, what are the things that you would recommend be described as out-of-scope?

198. Was planning completed before the Automation Readiness project was initiated?

199. Is your organization structure appropriate for the Automation Readiness projects size and complexity?

2.7 Assumption and Constraint Log: Automation Readiness

200. What weaknesses do you have?

201. Do documented requirements exist for all critical components and areas, including technical, business, interfaces, performance, security and conversion requirements?

202. Have you eliminated all duplicative tasks or manual efforts, where appropriate?

203. Have Automation Readiness project management standards and procedures been established and documented?

204. After observing execution of process, is it in compliance with the documented Plan?

205. Are processes for release management of new development from coding and unit testing, to integration testing, to training, and production defined and followed?

206. Are there processes in place to ensure that all the terms and code concepts have been documented consistently?

207. Are there cosmetic errors that hinder readability and comprehension?

208. Does the traceability documentation describe

the tool and/or mechanism to be used to capture traceability throughout the life cycle?

209. Have the scope, objectives, costs, benefits and impacts been communicated to all involved and/or impacted stakeholders and work groups?

210. Has a Automation Readiness project Communications Plan been developed?

211. Have all stakeholders been identified?

212. When can log be discarded?

213. What does an audit system look like?

214. Are formal code reviews conducted?

215. Are there procedures in place to effectively manage interdependencies with other Automation Readiness projects / systems?

216. Is there a Steering Committee in place?

217. Is the process working, and people are not executing in compliance of the process?

218. What strengths do you have?

2.8 Work Breakdown Structure: Automation Readiness

219. Can you make it?

220. How many levels?

221. When do you stop?

222. When does it have to be done?

223. Why would you develop a Work Breakdown Structure?

224. How big is a work-package?

225. Is the work breakdown structure (wbs) defined and is the scope of the Automation Readiness project clear with assigned deliverable owners?

226. Who has to do it?

227. Where does it take place?

228. How much detail?

229. Why is it useful?

230. What is the probability that the Automation Readiness project duration will exceed xx weeks?

231. Is it still viable?

232. How will you and your Automation Readiness project team define the Automation Readiness projects scope and work breakdown structure?

233. When would you develop a Work Breakdown Structure?

234. Is it a change in scope?

235. Do you need another level?

2.9 WBS Dictionary: Automation Readiness

236. Is all budget available as management reserve identified and excluded from the performance measurement baseline?

237. Are retroactive changes to BCWS and BCWP prohibited except for correction of errors or for normal accounting adjustments?

238. Time-phased control account budgets?

239. Are current work performance indicators and goals relatable to original goals as modified by contractual changes, replanning, and reprogramming actions?

240. Is undistributed budget limited to contract effort which cannot yet be planned to CWBS elements at or below the level specified for reporting to the Government?

241. Budgets assigned to major functional organizations?

242. Are work packages reasonably short in time duration or do they have adequate objective indicators/milestones to minimize subjectivity of the in process work evaluation?

243. Changes in the nature of the overhead requirements?

244. Are the rates for allocating costs from each indirect cost pool to contracts updated as necessary to ensure a realistic monthly allocation of indirect costs without significant year-end adjustments?

245. Is data disseminated to the contractors management timely, accurate, and usable?

246. Are records maintained to show how undistributed budgets are controlled?

247. Should you include sub-activities?

248. Are the contractors estimates of costs at completion reconcilable with cost data reported to us?

249. Are the requirements for all items of overhead established by rational, traceable processes?

250. Contractor financial periods; for example, annual?

251. Performance to date and material commitment?

252. Is budgeted cost for work performed calculated in a manner consistent with the way work is planned?

253. Are there procedures for monitoring action items and corrective actions to the point of resolution and are corresponding procedures being followed?

2.10 Schedule Management Plan: Automation Readiness

254. Has the budget been baselined?

255. Why time management?

256. Are schedule performance measures defined including pre-set triggers for specific actions?

257. Is the critical path valid?

258. What does a valid Schedule look like?

259. Has a structured approach been used to break work effort into manageable components (WBS)?

260. What is the estimated time to complete the Automation Readiness project if status quo is maintained?

261. Is there a formal process for updating the Automation Readiness project baseline?

262. Are all activities logically sequenced?

263. Is there a requirements change management processes in place?

264. Must the Automation Readiness project be complete by a specified date?

265. Are action items captured and managed?

266. Is there a procedure for management, control and release of schedule margin?

267. Are enough systems & user personnel assigned to the Automation Readiness project?

268. Why conduct schedule analysis?

269. Do Automation Readiness project teams & team members report on status / activities / progress?

270. Are all vendor contracts closed out?

271. How relevant is this attribute to this Automation Readiness project or audit?

272. Are written status reports provided on a designated frequent basis?

2.11 Activity List: Automation Readiness

273. In what sequence?

274. For other activities, how much delay can be tolerated?

275. What went wrong?

276. The wbs is developed as part of a joint planning session. and how do you know that youhave done this right?

277. What are the critical bottleneck activities?

278. Is there anything planned that does not need to be here?

279. What did not go as well?

280. What is the probability the Automation Readiness project can be completed in xx weeks?

281. What will be performed?

282. Can you determine the activity that must finish, before this activity can start?

283. Where will it be performed?

284. How can the Automation Readiness project be displayed graphically to better visualize the activities?

285. Are the required resources available or need to be acquired?

286. What went right?

287. Is infrastructure setup part of your Automation Readiness project?

288. How should ongoing costs be monitored to try to keep the Automation Readiness project within budget?

289. How much slack is available in the Automation Readiness project?

290. What is the total time required to complete the Automation Readiness project if no delays occur?

291. When do the individual activities need to start and finish?

2.12 Activity Attributes: Automation Readiness

292. How do you manage time?

293. Do you feel very comfortable with your prediction?

294. How difficult will it be to complete specific activities on this Automation Readiness project?

295. Activity: fair or not fair?

296. Is there a trend during the year?

297. Has management defined a definite timeframe for the turnaround or Automation Readiness project window?

298. Does your organization of the data change its meaning?

299. What is your organizations history in doing similar activities?

300. How else could the items be grouped?

301. Which method produces the more accurate cost assignment?

302. Resource is assigned to?

303. How much activity detail is required?

304. Activity: what is In the Bag?

305. Can you re-assign any activities to another resource to resolve an over-allocation?

306. What is missing?

307. Why?

308. How difficult will it be to do specific activities on this Automation Readiness project?

309. What activity do you think you should spend the most time on?

2.13 Milestone List: Automation Readiness

310. Timescales, deadlines and pressures?

311. Identify critical paths (one or more) and which activities are on the critical path?

312. Marketing - reach, distribution, awareness?

313. Information and research?

314. Describe the concept of the technology, product or service that will be or has been developed. How will it be used?

315. Do you foresee any technical risks or developmental challenges?

316. It is to be a narrative text providing the crucial aspects of your Automation Readiness project proposal answering what, who, how, when and where?

317. What background experience, skills, and strengths does the team bring to your organization?

318. Insurmountable weaknesses?

319. Reliability of data, plan predictability?

320. Level of the Innovation?

321. What is the market for your technology, product or service?

322. How soon can the activity start?

323. Sustaining internal capabilities?

324. What specific improvements did you make to the Automation Readiness project proposal since the previous time?

325. Calculate how long can activity be delayed?

326. When will the Automation Readiness project be complete?

327. Environmental effects?

328. What has been done so far?

2.14 Network Diagram: Automation Readiness

329. What is the completion time?

330. Which type of network diagram allows you to depict four types of dependencies?

331. Are you on time?

332. Review the logical flow of the network diagram. Take a look at which activities you have first and then sequence the activities. Do they make sense?

333. What job or jobs follow it?

334. If the Automation Readiness project network diagram cannot change and you have extra personnel resources, what is the BEST thing to do?

335. What activities must follow this activity?

336. Where do schedules come from?

337. What are the Key Success Factors?

338. If a current contract exists, can you provide the vendor name, contract start, and contract expiration date?

339. What are the tools?

340. Can you calculate the confidence level?

341. What job or jobs could run concurrently?

342. What controls the start and finish of a job?

343. Planning: who, how long, what to do?

344. Why must you schedule milestones, such as reviews, throughout the Automation Readiness project?

345. What must be completed before an activity can be started?

2.15 Activity Resource Requirements: Automation Readiness

346. Why do you do that?

347. Other support in specific areas?

348. Do you use tools like decomposition and rolling-wave planning to produce the activity list and other outputs?

349. Which logical relationship does the PDM use most often?

350. What is the Work Plan Standard?

351. What are constraints that you might find during the Human Resource Planning process?

352. How many signatures do you require on a check and does this match what is in your policy and procedures?

353. Organizational Applicability?

354. How do you handle petty cash?

355. Anything else?

356. Time for overtime?

357. When does monitoring begin?

358. Are there unresolved issues that need to be addressed?

2.16 Resource Breakdown Structure: Automation Readiness

359. When do they need the information?

360. Is predictive resource analysis being done?

361. Which resources should be in the resource pool?

362. How difficult will it be to do specific activities on this Automation Readiness project?

363. What is Automation Readiness project communication management?

364. What is the difference between % Complete and % work?

365. What defines a successful Automation Readiness project?

366. What are the requirements for resource data?

367. Why do you do it?

368. What can you do to improve productivity?

369. Why is this important?

370. Changes based on input from stakeholders?

371. What is the purpose of assigning and documenting responsibility?

372. Which resource planning tool provides information on resource responsibility and accountability?

373. Who will be used as a Automation Readiness project team member?

2.17 Activity Duration Estimates: Automation Readiness

374. What are some general rules of thumb for deciding if cost variance, schedule variance, cost performance index, and schedule performance index numbers are good or bad?

375. What is done after activity duration estimation?

376. See what went wrong?

377. Who will promote it?

378. Who will be the main sponsor for it?

379. Do you think Automation Readiness project managers of large information technology Automation Readiness projects need strong technical skills?

380. Are Automation Readiness project activities decomposed into manageable components to ensure expected management control?

381. Are inspections completed to determine if the results comply with the requirements?

382. Which types of reports would help provide summary information to senior management?

383. What is the duration of the critical path for this Automation Readiness project?

384. If you plan to take the PMP exam soon, what should you do to prepare?

385. How does poking fun at technical professionals communications skills impact the industry and educational programs?

386. Does the case present a realistic scenario?

387. List five reasons why organizations outsource. Why is there a growing trend in outsourcing, especially in the government?

388. Are operational definitions created to identify quality measurement criteria for specific activities?

389. What are crucial elements of successful Automation Readiness project plan execution?

390. Are risks monitored to determine if an event has occurred or if the mitigation was successful?

391. Do they make sense?

392. How is the Automation Readiness project doing?

2.18 Duration Estimating Worksheet: Automation Readiness

393. What info is needed?

394. What is cost and Automation Readiness project cost management?

395. Define the work as completely as possible. What work will be included in the Automation Readiness project?

396. What utility impacts are there?

397. Do any colleagues have experience with your organization and/or RFPs?

398. What questions do you have?

399. When, then?

400. Is the Automation Readiness project responsive to community need?

401. Done before proceeding with this activity or what can be done concurrently?

402. When does your organization expect to be able to complete it?

403. Is this operation cost effective?

404. Science = process: remember the scientific

method?

405. How should ongoing costs be monitored to try to keep the Automation Readiness project within budget?

406. Can the Automation Readiness project be constructed as planned?

407. Will the Automation Readiness project collaborate with the local community and leverage resources?

408. What is the total time required to complete the Automation Readiness project if no delays occur?

2.19 Project Schedule: Automation Readiness

409. How detailed should a Automation Readiness project get?

410. Is infrastructure setup part of your Automation Readiness project?

411. Why or why not?

412. How do you manage Automation Readiness project Risk?

413. Change management required?

414. Why do you need to manage Automation Readiness project Risk?

415. Why is software Automation Readiness project disaster so common?

416. Are quality inspections and review activities listed in the Automation Readiness project schedule(s)?

417. How can you address that situation?

418. How effectively were issues able to be resolved without impacting the Automation Readiness project Schedule or Budget?

419. Does the condition or event threaten the

Automation Readiness projects objectives in any ways?

420. Your Automation Readiness project management plan results in a Automation Readiness project schedule that is too long. If the Automation Readiness project network diagram cannot change and you have extra personnel resources, what is the BEST thing to do?

421. Is the structure for tracking the Automation Readiness project schedule well defined and assigned to a specific individual?

422. Why do you need schedules?

423. Understand the constraints used in preparing the schedule. Are activities connected because logic dictates the order in which others occur?

424. Are procedures defined by which the Automation Readiness project schedule may be changed?

425. Month Automation Readiness project take?

426. If there are any qualifying green components to this Automation Readiness project, what portion of the total Automation Readiness project cost is green?

2.20 Cost Management Plan: Automation Readiness

427. Are key risk mitigation strategies added to the Automation Readiness project schedule?

428. Does the schedule include Automation Readiness project management time and change request analysis time?

429. Forecasts – how will the time and resources needed to complete the Automation Readiness project be forecast?

430. For cost control purposes?

431. Were stakeholders aware and supportive of the principles and practices of modern software estimation?

432. Is an industry recognized mechanized support tool(s) being used for Automation Readiness project scheduling & tracking?

433. Are procurement deliverables arriving on time and to specification?

434. Are there checklists created to determine if all quality processes are followed?

435. Cost tracking and performance analysis – How will cost tracking and performance analysis be accomplished?

436. Exclusions – is there scope to be performed or provided by others?

437. Is quality monitored from the perspective of the customers needs and expectations?

438. Are decisions captured in a decisions log?

439. Best practices implementation – How will change management be applied to this Automation Readiness project?

440. Are vendor contract reports, reviews and visits conducted periodically?

441. Who will prepare the cost estimates?

442. Are assumptions being identified, recorded, analyzed, qualified and closed?

443. Have adequate resources been provided by management to ensure Automation Readiness project success?

444. Are quality inspections and review activities listed in the Automation Readiness project schedule(s)?

2.21 Activity Cost Estimates: Automation Readiness

445. How do you change activities?

446. What procedures are put in place regarding bidding and cost comparisons, if any?

447. Does the estimator have experience?

448. Is costing method consistent with study goals?

449. What is procurement?

450. How do you do activity recasts?

451. Were decisions made in a timely manner?

452. Will you need to provide essential services information about activities?

453. Review – what are some common errors in activities to avoid?

454. What are the audit requirements?

455. Why do you manage cost?

456. How many activities should you have?

457. Was the consultant knowledgeable about the program?

458. Can you delete activities or make them inactive?

459. Performance bond should always provide what part of the contract value?

460. What makes a good activity description?

461. The impact and what actions were taken?

462. Eac -estimate at completion, what is the total job expected to cost?

463. Are cost subtotals needed?

464. Padding is bad and contingencies are good. what is the difference?

2.22 Cost Estimating Worksheet: Automation Readiness

465. Ask: are others positioned to know, are others credible, and will others cooperate?

466. Identify the timeframe necessary to monitor progress and collect data to determine how the selected measure has changed?

467. Who is best positioned to know and assist in identifying corresponding factors?

468. What additional Automation Readiness project(s) could be initiated as a result of this Automation Readiness project?

469. Can a trend be established from historical performance data on the selected measure and are the criteria for using trend analysis or forecasting methods met?

470. How will the results be shared and to whom?

471. What will others want?

472. Will the Automation Readiness project collaborate with the local community and leverage resources?

473. Does the Automation Readiness project provide innovative ways for stakeholders to overcome obstacles or deliver better outcomes?

474. What can be included?

475. What costs are to be estimated?

476. What is the estimated labor cost today based upon this information?

477. What happens to any remaining funds not used?

478. Is the Automation Readiness project responsive to community need?

479. Value pocket identification & quantification what are value pockets?

480. What is the purpose of estimating?

481. Is it feasible to establish a control group arrangement?

2.23 Cost Baseline: Automation Readiness

482. Does a process exist for establishing a cost baseline to measure Automation Readiness project performance?

483. Has operations management formally accepted responsibility for operating and maintaining the product(s) or service(s) delivered by the Automation Readiness project?

484. Does the suggested change request represent a desired enhancement to the products functionality?

485. Has the appropriate access to relevant data and analysis capability been granted?

486. What deliverables come first?

487. Automation Readiness project goals -should others be reconsidered?

488. Review your risk triggers -have your risks changed?

489. How accurate do cost estimates need to be?

490. Does the suggested change request seem to represent a necessary enhancement to the product?

491. What threats might prevent you from getting there?

492. Have the lessons learned been filed with the Automation Readiness project Management Office?

493. Pcs for your new business. what would the life cycle costs be?

494. At which frequency ?

495. Have all approved changes to the cost baseline been identified and impact on the Automation Readiness project documented?

496. Are you asking management for something as a result of this update?

497. On time?

498. For what purpose ?

2.24 Quality Management Plan: Automation Readiness

499. Do the data quality objectives communicate the intended program need?

500. How are new requirements or changes to requirements identified?

501. List your organizations customer contact standards that employees are expected to maintain. How are corresponding standards measured?

502. How relevant is this attribute to this Automation Readiness project or audit?

503. Is a component/condition present?

504. What are your organizations current levels and trends for the already stated measures related to financial and marketplace performance?

505. What data do you gather/use/compile?

506. How is staff trained in procedures?

507. How is equipment calibrated?

508. How does your organization measure customer satisfaction/dissatisfaction?

509. How do you ensure that protocols are up to date?

510. What is quality and how will you ensure it?

511. Does the program use modeling in the permitting or decision-making processes?

512. What are your organizations current levels and trends for the already stated measures related to employee wellbeing, satisfaction, and development?

513. Have all involved stakeholders and work groups committed to the Automation Readiness project?

514. How does your organization establish and maintain customer relationships?

515. How does the material compare to a regulatory threshold?

516. Are you meeting your customers expectations consistently?

517. What field records are generated?

2.25 Quality Metrics: Automation Readiness

518. Who is willing to lead?

519. Are quality metrics defined?

520. What do you measure?

521. How do you know if everyone is trying to improve the right things?

522. When is the security analysis testing complete?

523. What makes a visualization memorable?

524. Was the overall quality better or worse than previous products?

525. Do you stratify metrics by product or site?

526. How do you calculate corresponding metrics?

527. Where is quality now?

528. What method of measurement do you use?

529. Was review conducted per standard protocols?

530. What documentation is required?

531. How do you measure?

532. How should customers provide input?

533. What percentage are outcome-based?

534. What are your organizations expectations for its quality Automation Readiness project?

535. The metrics–what is being considered?

2.26 Process Improvement Plan: Automation Readiness

536. Purpose of goal: the motive is determined by asking, why do you want to achieve this goal?

537. Are you making progress on the improvement framework?

538. Has a process guide to collect the data been developed?

539. If a process improvement framework is being used, which elements will help the problems and goals listed?

540. Why quality management?

541. Does your process ensure quality?

542. Have the supporting tools been developed or acquired?

543. What personnel are the champions for the initiative?

544. Have the frequency of collection and the points in the process where measurements will be made been determined?

545. Are you meeting the quality standards?

546. Where do you want to be?

547. Modeling current processes is great, and will you ever see a return on that investment?

548. How do you manage quality?

549. What personnel are the change agents for your initiative?

550. Everyone agrees on what process improvement is, right?

551. What is the test-cycle concept?

552. Are you making progress on the goals?

553. Where are you now?

554. What is the return on investment?

2.27 Responsibility Assignment Matrix: Automation Readiness

555. Is accountability placed at the lowest-possible level within the Automation Readiness project so that decisions can be made at that level?

556. Changes in the current direct and Automation Readiness projected base?

557. Past experience – the person or the group worked at something similar in the past?

558. Are all elements of indirect expense identified to overhead cost budgets of Automation Readiness projections?

559. Are your organizations and items of cost assigned to each pool identified?

560. Are indirect costs accumulated for comparison with the corresponding budgets?

561. Cwbs elements to be subcontracted, with identification of subcontractors?

562. Identify potential or actual overruns and underruns?

563. Identify and isolate causes of favorable and unfavorable cost and schedule variances?

564. What materials and procurements needed?

565. Evaluate the impact of schedule changes, work around, etc?

566. Does the contractors system include procedures for measuring the performance of critical subcontractors?

567. Does the contractor use objective results, design reviews and tests to trace schedule performance?

568. Are others working on the right things?

569. Do you need to convince people that its well worth the time and effort?

570. Who is the sponsor?

571. Why cost benefit analysis?

572. What expertise is available in your department?

573. What is the business need?

2.28 Roles and Responsibilities: Automation Readiness

574. Implementation of actions: Who are the responsible units?

575. Required skills, knowledge, experience?

576. Where are you most strong as a supervisor?

577. Was the expectation clearly communicated?

578. What should you highlight for improvement?

579. What areas of supervision are challenging for you?

580. What expectations were met?

581. Who is responsible for each task?

582. Concern: where are you limited or have no authority, where you can not influence?

583. Does the team have access to and ability to use data analysis tools?

584. Are governance roles and responsibilities documented?

585. What is working well?

586. What is working well within your organizations

performance management system?

587. What specific behaviors did you observe?

588. What should you do now to ensure that you are exceeding expectations and excelling in your current position?

589. What expectations were NOT met?

590. What are your major roles and responsibilities in the area of performance measurement and assessment?

591. Once the responsibilities are defined for the Automation Readiness project, have the deliverables, roles and responsibilities been clearly communicated to every participant?

2.29 Human Resource Management Plan: Automation Readiness

592. Are the key elements of a Automation Readiness project Charter present?

593. Is this Automation Readiness project carried out in partnership with other groups/organizations?

594. Are all resource assumptions documented?

595. Is a payment system in place with proper reviews and approvals?

596. Are there dependencies with other initiatives or Automation Readiness projects?

597. Have lessons learned been conducted after each Automation Readiness project release?

598. Who needs training?

599. Have reserves been created to address risks?

600. How relevant is this attribute to this Automation Readiness project or audit?

601. Is there a formal process for updating the Automation Readiness project baseline?

602. Has your organization readiness assessment been conducted?

603. Are schedule deliverables actually delivered?

604. Are target dates established for each milestone deliverable?

605. Are people motivated to meet the current and future challenges?

606. Has a quality assurance plan been developed for the Automation Readiness project?

607. Do Automation Readiness project teams & team members report on status / activities / progress?

608. Have all necessary approvals been obtained?

609. Did the Automation Readiness project team have the right skills?

2.30 Communications Management Plan: Automation Readiness

610. How were corresponding initiatives successful?

611. Who did you turn to if you had questions?

612. Are others part of the communications management plan?

613. Are there common objectives between the team and the stakeholder?

614. What data is going to be required?

615. In your work, how much time is spent on stakeholder identification?

616. Who will use or be affected by the result of a Automation Readiness project?

617. Are stakeholders internal or external?

618. Is the stakeholder role recognized by your organization?

619. What to learn?

620. Do you feel a register helps?

621. What to know?

622. Are there potential barriers between the team

and the stakeholder?

623. Who to learn from?

624. What approaches do you use?

625. Timing: when do the effects of the communication take place?

626. Why do you manage communications?

627. How is this initiative related to other portfolios, programs, or Automation Readiness projects?

628. Where do team members get information?

2.31 Risk Management Plan: Automation Readiness

629. What things are likely to change?

630. What can you do to minimize the impact if it does?

631. How can you fix it?

632. Workarounds are determined during which step of risk management?

633. Are you working on the right risks?

634. Have top software and customer managers formally committed to support the Automation Readiness project?

635. Are end-users enthusiastically committed to the Automation Readiness project and the system/ product to be built?

636. How risk averse are you?

637. Is the number of people on the Automation Readiness project team adequate to do the job?

638. Are team members trained in the use of the tools?

639. Are there risks to human health or the environment that need to be controlled or mitigated?

640. Are some people working on multiple Automation Readiness projects?

641. Which risks should get the attention?

642. Has something like this been done before?

643. Havent software Automation Readiness projects been late before?

644. Have customers been involved fully in the definition of requirements?

645. Is there anything you would now do differently on your Automation Readiness project based on this experience?

646. How is implementation of risk actions performed?

647. Does the Automation Readiness project have the authority and ability to avoid the risk?

648. Which is an input to the risk management process?

2.32 Risk Register: Automation Readiness

649. User involvement: do you have the right users?

650. Why would you develop a risk register?

651. Do you require further engagement?

652. Are there any knock-on effects/impact on any of the other areas?

653. What is a Community Risk Register?

654. What are your key risks/show istoppers and what is being done to manage them?

655. What is a Risk?

656. What is the reason for current performance gaps and do the risks and opportunities identified previously account for this?

657. Who is accountable?

658. What action, if any, has been taken to respond to the risk?

659. Severity Prediction?

660. What are you going to do to limit the Automation Readiness projects risk exposure due to the identified risks?

661. What may happen or not go according to plan?

662. What are the main aims, objectives of the policy, strategy, or service and the intended outcomes?

663. What should you do now?

664. What are the major risks facing the Automation Readiness project?

665. What is the probability and impact of the risk occurring?

666. Is further information required before making a decision?

667. Risk probability and impact: how will the probabilities and impacts of risk items be assessed?

2.33 Probability and Impact Assessment: Automation Readiness

668. Are the software tools integrated with each other?

669. What are the chances the risk event will occur?

670. Are testing tools available and suitable?

671. My Automation Readiness project leader has suddenly left your organization, what do you do?

672. Risk data quality assessment - what is the quality of the data used to determine or assess the risk?

673. Can this technology be absorbed with current level of expertise available in your organization?

674. Costs associated with late delivery or a defective product?

675. What are the likely future requirements?

676. Monitoring of the overall Automation Readiness project status – are there any changes in the Automation Readiness project that can effect and cause new possible risks?

677. Are tool mentors available?

678. Assuming that you have identified a number of risks in the Automation Readiness project, how would

you prioritize them?

679. Are the risk data complete?

680. Is the Automation Readiness project cutting across the entire organization?

681. What things might go wrong?

682. Can you stabilize dynamic risk factors?

683. Are flexibility and reuse paramount?

684. What are the preparations required for facing difficulties?

685. What are the uncertainties associated with the technology selected for the Automation Readiness project?

686. Are some people working on multiple Automation Readiness projects?

687. Risks should be identified during which phase of Automation Readiness project management life cycle?

2.34 Probability and Impact Matrix: Automation Readiness

688. How solid are the price-volume Automation Readiness projections?

689. To what extent is the chosen technology maturing?

690. Do you know the order of planning yet?

691. How are the local factors going to affect the absorption?

692. What are the chances the event will occur?

693. Can the Automation Readiness project proceed without assuming the risk?

694. What will be the likely incidence of conflict with neighboring Automation Readiness projects?

695. What is the level of commitment and professionalism?

696. How much risk do others need to take?

697. What are the current or emerging trends of culture?

698. How likely is the current plan to come in on schedule or on budget?

699. What is the likely future demand of the customer?

700. Can it be changed quickly?

701. Mitigation -how can you avoid the risk?

702. What should you do FIRST?

703. How do risks change during the Automation Readiness projects life cycle?

704. Is the process supported by tools?

2.35 Risk Data Sheet: Automation Readiness

705. What are you weak at and therefore need to do better?

706. Potential for recurrence?

707. What is the chance that it will happen?

708. Do effective diagnostic tests exist?

709. Is the data sufficiently specified in terms of the type of failure being analyzed, and its frequency or probability?

710. Risk of what?

711. Are new hazards created?

712. How can hazards be reduced?

713. What is the likelihood of it happening?

714. Whom do you serve (customers)?

715. What are you here for (Mission)?

716. How reliable is the data source?

717. Has a sensitivity analysis been carried out?

718. What were the Causes that contributed?

719. During work activities could hazards exist?

720. Has the most cost-effective solution been chosen?

721. What was measured?

722. What if client refuses?

723. What do people affected think about the need for, and practicality of preventive measures?

724. What will be the consequences if the risk happens?

2.36 Procurement Management Plan: Automation Readiness

725. Are risk triggers captured?

726. What are your quality assurance overheads?

727. Is there a formal set of procedures supporting Stakeholder Management?

728. Are internal Automation Readiness project status meetings held at reasonable intervals?

729. Was the Automation Readiness project schedule reviewed by all stakeholders and formally accepted?

730. Measurable - are the targets measurable?

731. Do all stakeholders know how to access the PM repository and where to find the Automation Readiness project documentation?

732. Is the structure for tracking the Automation Readiness project schedule well defined and assigned to a specific individual?

733. Do Automation Readiness project teams & team members report on status / activities / progress?

734. Published materials?

735. Have the key elements of a coherent Automation Readiness project management strategy been

established?

736. What areas does the group agree are the biggest success on the Automation Readiness project?

737. Are post milestone Automation Readiness project reviews (PMPR) conducted with your organization at least once a year?

738. Have key stakeholders been identified?

739. Does all Automation Readiness project documentation reside in a common repository for easy access?

740. Have all team members been part of identifying risks?

2.37 Source Selection Criteria: Automation Readiness

741. When is it appropriate to issue a DRFP?

742. Are types/quantities of material, facilities appropriate?

743. What are the requirements for publicizing a RFP?

744. What should a Draft Request for Proposal (DRFP) include?

745. With the rapid changes in information technology, will media be readable in five or ten years?

746. Is experience evaluated?

747. How should comments received in response to a RFP be handled?

748. Do you have a plan to document consensus results including disposition of any disagreement by individual evaluators?

749. How much past performance information should be requested?

750. What does a sample rating scale look like?

751. Who is on the Source Selection Advisory Committee?

752. How should the solicitation aspects regarding past performance be structured?

753. How is past performance evaluated?

754. What is the basis of an estimate and what assumptions were made?

755. What are open book debriefings?

756. What is the role of counsel in the procurement process?

757. How are oral presentations documented?

758. What are the special considerations for preaward debriefings?

759. Does your documentation identify why the team concurs or differs with reported performance from past performance report (CPARs, questionnaire responses, etc.)?

760. Is the contracting office likely to receive more purchase requests for this item or service during the coming year?

2.38 Stakeholder Management Plan: Automation Readiness

761. Is there a set of procedures defining the scope, procedures, and deliverables defining quality control?

762. How are stakeholders chosen and what roles might they have on a Automation Readiness project?

763. Have activity relationships and interdependencies within tasks been adequately identified?

764. Who will be responsible for managing and maintaining the Issues Register?

765. Will all outputs delivered by the Automation Readiness project follow the same process?

766. Have the key elements of a coherent Automation Readiness project management strategy been established?

767. Can the requirements be traced to the appropriate components of the solution, as well as test scripts?

768. Are best practices and metrics employed to identify issues, progress, performance, etc.?

769. Has a capability assessment been conducted?

770. Will the current technology alter during the life of

the Automation Readiness project?

771. Are enough systems & user personnel assigned to the Automation Readiness project?

772. What potential impact does the stakeholder have on the Automation Readiness project?

773. Are risk oriented checklists used during risk identification?

774. Will all relevant stakeholders be included within the review process?

775. What is the primary function of the Activity Decomposition Decision Tree?

776. Is documentation created for communication with the suppliers and vendors?

777. What is the difference between product and Automation Readiness project scope?

778. Are the payment terms being followed?

779. What methods are to be used for managing and monitoring subcontractors (eg agreements, contracts etc)?

2.39 Change Management Plan: Automation Readiness

780. Who might present the most resistance?

781. What does a resilient organization look like?

782. Is there a support model for this application and are the details available for distribution?

783. How many people are required in each of the roles?

784. When should a given message be communicated?

785. What will be the preferred method of delivery?

786. What did the people around you say about it?

787. Has the training co-ordinator been provided with the training details and put in place the necessary arrangements?

788. When does it make sense to customize?

789. What are the current methods of sharing information and do there need to be new ones developed?

790. What method and medium would you use to announce a message?

791. What is the most cynical response it can receive?

792. What risks may occur upfront?

793. Who in the business it includes?

794. When to start change management?

795. Who might be able to help you the most?

796. What time commitment will this involve?

797. Would you need to tailor a special message for each segment of the audience?

798. What are the needs, priorities and special interests of the audience?

799. What type of materials/channels will be available to leverage?

3.0 Executing Process Group: Automation Readiness

800. Why should Automation Readiness project managers strive to make jobs look easy?

801. On which process should team members spend the most time?

802. Were sponsors and decision makers available when needed outside regularly scheduled meetings?

803. What is the shortest possible time it will take to complete this Automation Readiness project?

804. If action is called for, what form should it take?

805. Could a new application negatively affect the current IT infrastructure?

806. Who will provide training?

807. What Automation Readiness projects and services are in the portfolio of your organization?

808. After how many days will the lease cost be the same as the purchase cost for the equipment?

809. Does the Automation Readiness project team have enough people to execute the Automation Readiness project plan?

810. Would you rate yourself as being risk-averse, risk-

neutral, or risk-seeking?

811. Based on your Automation Readiness project communication management plan, what worked well?

812. Are escalated issues resolved promptly?

813. Is the Automation Readiness project making progress in helping to achieve the set results?

814. What were things that you did very well and want to do the same again on the next Automation Readiness project?

815. How could you control progress of your Automation Readiness project?

816. How well defined and documented were the Automation Readiness project management processes you chose to use?

817. How do you enter durations, link tasks, and view critical path information?

818. What are some crucial elements of a good Automation Readiness project plan?

819. Why do you need a good WBS to use Automation Readiness project management software?

3.1 Team Member Status Report: Automation Readiness

820. How will resource planning be done?

821. Why is it to be done?

822. Are the products of your organizations Automation Readiness projects meeting customers objectives?

823. The problem with Reward & Recognition Programs is that the truly deserving people all too often get left out. How can you make it practical?

824. What is to be done?

825. Does your organization have the means (staff, money, contract, etc.) to produce or to acquire the product, good, or service?

826. Do you have an Enterprise Automation Readiness project Management Office (EPMO)?

827. Does the product, good, or service already exist within your organization?

828. When a teams productivity and success depend on collaboration and the efficient flow of information, what generally fails them?

829. How much risk is involved?

830. How does this product, good, or service meet the needs of the Automation Readiness project and your organization as a whole?

831. Does every department have to have a Automation Readiness project Manager on staff?

832. Are the attitudes of staff regarding Automation Readiness project work improving?

833. How it is to be done?

834. How can you make it practical?

835. Will the staff do training or is that done by a third party?

836. What specific interest groups do you have in place?

837. Is there evidence that staff is taking a more professional approach toward management of your organizations Automation Readiness projects?

838. Are your organizations Automation Readiness projects more successful over time?

3.2 Change Request: Automation Readiness

839. Can you answer what happened, who did it, when did it happen, and what else will be affected?

840. Will new change requests be acknowledged in a timely manner?

841. Are there requirements attributes that are strongly related to the complexity and size?

842. Why control change across the life cycle?

843. How shall the implementation of changes be recorded?

844. Why do you want to have a change control system?

845. Has your address changed?

846. Who is responsible to authorize changes?

847. What type of changes does change control take into account?

848. Which requirements attributes affect the risk to reliability the most?

849. Customer acceptance plan how will the customer verify the change has been implemented successfully?

850. Who is included in the change control team?

851. What has an inspector to inspect and to check?

852. Is it feasible to use requirements attributes as predictors of reliability?

853. When to submit a change request?

854. What must be taken into consideration when introducing change control programs?

855. Will there be a change request form in use?

856. Since there are no change requests in your Automation Readiness project at this point, what must you have before you begin?

857. Have scm procedures for noting the change, recording it, and reporting it been followed?

858. Should staff call into the helpdesk or go to the website?

3.3 Change Log: Automation Readiness

859. Is the requested change request a result of changes in other Automation Readiness project(s)?

860. Do the described changes impact on the integrity or security of the system?

861. How does this change affect the timeline of the schedule?

862. Is the change backward compatible without limitations?

863. How does this relate to the standards developed for specific business processes?

864. Is the submitted change a new change or a modification of a previously approved change?

865. Where do changes come from?

866. Is the change request open, closed or pending?

867. Should a more thorough impact analysis be conducted?

868. How does this change affect scope?

869. Who initiated the change request?

870. Is this a mandatory replacement?

871. Is the change request within Automation Readiness project scope?

872. When was the request approved?

873. Will the Automation Readiness project fail if the change request is not executed?

874. When was the request submitted?

3.4 Decision Log: Automation Readiness

875. Meeting purpose; why does this team meet?

876. It becomes critical to track and periodically revisit both operational effectiveness; Are you noticing all that you need to, and are you interpreting what you see effectively?

877. What was the rationale for the decision?

878. What eDiscovery problem or issue did your organization set out to fix or make better?

879. What alternatives/risks were considered?

880. Linked to original objective?

881. Is your opponent open to a non-traditional workflow, or will it likely challenge anything you do?

882. Is everything working as expected?

883. What makes you different or better than others companies selling the same thing?

884. How do you define success?

885. With whom was the decision shared or considered?

886. Decision-making process; how will the team

make decisions?

887. What is your overall strategy for quality control / quality assurance procedures?

888. What are the cost implications?

889. What is the average size of your matters in an applicable measurement?

890. What is the line where eDiscovery ends and document review begins?

891. How does provision of information, both in terms of content and presentation, influence acceptance of alternative strategies?

892. Behaviors; what are guidelines that the team has identified that will assist them with getting the most out of team meetings?

893. How consolidated and comprehensive a story can you tell by capturing currently available incident data in a central location and through a log of key decisions during an incident?

894. Adversarial environment. is your opponent open to a non-traditional workflow, or will it likely challenge anything you do?

3.5 Quality Audit: Automation Readiness

895. What mechanisms exist for identification of staff development needs?

896. How do you know what, specifically, is required of you in your work?

897. How does your organization know that its system for supporting staff research capability is appropriately effective and constructive?

898. How does your organization know that its system for recruiting the best staff possible are appropriately effective and constructive?

899. Quality is about improvement and accountability. The immediate questions that arise out of that statement are: (i) improvement on what, and (ii) accountable to whom?

900. Can your organization demonstrate exactly how and why results were achieved?

901. What is your organizations greatest strength?

902. How does your organization know that its planning processes are appropriately effective and constructive?

903. How does your organization know that its management system is appropriately effective and

constructive?

904. Are measuring and test equipment that have been placed out of service suitably identified and excluded from use in any device reconditioning operation?

905. Are all employees including salespersons made aware that they must report all complaints received from any source for inclusion in the complaint handling system?

906. How does your organization know that its risk management system is appropriately effective and constructive?

907. What does an analysis of your organizations staff profile suggest in terms of its planning, and how is this being addressed?

908. Statements of intent remain exactly that until they are put into effect. The next step is to deploy the already stated intentions. In other words, do the plans happen in reality?

909. How does your organization know that its staff embody the core knowledge, skills and characteristics for which it wishes to be recognized?

910. What are the main things that hinder your ability to do a good job?

911. Health and safety arrangements; stress management workshops. How does your organization know that it provides a safe and healthy environment?

912. Is the reports overall tone appropriate?

913. How do staff know if they are doing a good job?

3.6 Team Directory: Automation Readiness

914. How will the team handle changes?

915. Why is the work necessary?

916. Who will talk to the customer?

917. Who are the Team Members?

918. Where will the product be used and/or delivered or built when appropriate?

919. Process decisions: how well was task order work performed?

920. How does the team resolve conflicts and ensure tasks are completed?

921. Process decisions: is work progressing on schedule and per contract requirements?

922. Have you decided when to celebrate the Automation Readiness projects completion date?

923. Decisions: what could be done better to improve the quality of the constructed product?

924. Process decisions: are all start-up, turn over and close out requirements of the contract satisfied?

925. Does a Automation Readiness project team

directory list all resources assigned to the Automation Readiness project?

926. Process decisions: are there any statutory or regulatory issues relevant to the timely execution of work?

927. How and in what format should information be presented?

928. What needs to be communicated?

929. Contract requirements complied with?

930. Days from the time the issue is identified?

931. Timing: when do the effects of communication take place?

3.7 Team Operating Agreement: Automation Readiness

932. Do you vary your voice pace, tone and pitch to engage participants and gain involvement?

933. Have you set the goals and objectives of the team?

934. Communication protocols: how will the team communicate?

935. What are the boundaries (organizational or geographic) within which you operate?

936. Did you draft the meeting agenda?

937. Are there more than two functional areas represented by your team?

938. Does your team need access to all documents and information at all times?

939. Do you call or email participants to ensure understanding, follow-through and commitment to the meeting outcomes?

940. Methodologies: how will key team processes be implemented, such as training, research, work deliverable production, review and approval processes, knowledge management, and meeting procedures?

941. Do you send out the agenda and meeting materials in advance?

942. How will you resolve conflict efficiently and respectfully?

943. Seconds for members to respond?

944. What individual strengths does each team member bring to the group?

945. Do you brief absent members after they view meeting notes or listen to a recording?

946. Do you record meetings for the already stated unable to attend?

947. Did you recap the meeting purpose, time, and expectations?

948. Conflict resolution: how will disputes and other conflicts be mediated or resolved?

949. Do you post meeting notes and the recording (if used) and notify participants?

950. Is compensation based on team and individual performance?

951. What are some potential sources of conflict among team members?

3.8 Team Performance Assessment: Automation Readiness

952. How hard did you try to make a good selection?

953. Effects of crew composition on crew performance: Does the whole equal the sum of its parts?

954. What is method variance?

955. To what degree will the team adopt a concrete, clearly understood, and agreed-upon approach that will result in achievement of the teams goals?

956. When does the medium matter?

957. Lack of method variance in self-reported affect and perceptions at work: Reality or artifact?

958. To what degree are the teams goals and objectives clear, simple, and measurable?

959. Do you give group members authority to make at least some important decisions?

960. To what degree can team members frequently and easily communicate with one another?

961. Where to from here?

962. To what degree are staff involved as partners in the improvement process?

963. To what degree are fresh input and perspectives systematically caught and added (for example, through information and analysis, new members, and senior sponsors)?

964. To what degree can the team measure progress against specific goals?

965. To what degree is the team cognizant of small wins to be celebrated along the way?

966. Which situations call for a more extreme type of adaptiveness in which team members actually re-define roles?

967. How hard do you try to make a good selection?

968. How do you recognize and praise members for contributions?

969. How do you keep key people outside the group informed about its accomplishments?

970. To what degree are the goals ambitious?

971. To what degree will the approach capitalize on and enhance the skills of all team members in a manner that takes into consideration other demands on members of the team?

3.9 Team Member Performance Assessment: Automation Readiness

972. How are training activities developed from a technical perspective?

973. What future plans (e.g., modifications) do you have for your program?

974. To what degree do team members articulate the teams work approach?

975. Is it critical or vital to the job?

976. What is the target group for instruction (e.g., individual and collective or small team instruction)?

977. What is the large, desired outcome?

978. Does the rater (supervisor) have the authority or responsibility to tell an employee that the employees performance is unsatisfactory?

979. Are any governance changes sufficient to impact achievement?

980. To what degree does the teams approach to its work allow for modification and improvement over time?

981. How do you work together to improve teaching and learning?

982. Does adaptive training work?

983. What evaluation results do you have?

984. How do you start collaborating?

985. Are assessment validation activities performed?

986. Are any validation activities performed?

987. How does your team work together?

988. In what areas would you like to concentrate your knowledge and resources?

989. Why do performance reviews?

990. What is the role of the Reviewer?

3.10 Issue Log: Automation Readiness

991. How much time does it take to do it?

992. Are you constantly rushing from meeting to meeting?

993. Is access to the Issue Log controlled?

994. Why do you manage human resources?

995. Are the stakeholders getting the information they need, are they consulted, are concerns addressed?

996. Which stakeholders can influence others?

997. Are the Automation Readiness project issues uniquely identified, including to which product they refer?

998. Do you have members of your team responsible for certain stakeholders?

999. Which stakeholders are thought leaders, influences, or early adopters?

1000. Who is the issue assigned to?

1001. How do you reply to this question; you am new here and managing this major program. How do you suggest you build your network?

1002. What is the impact on the Business Case?

1003. How do you manage communications?

1004. Who is the stakeholder?

1005. Why multiple evaluators?

1006. In classifying stakeholders, which approach to do so are you using?

1007. What effort will a change need?

1008. What is the status of the issue?

4.0 Monitoring and Controlling Process Group: Automation Readiness

1009. How are you doing?

1010. Is the program in place as intended?

1011. Is there sufficient time allotted between the general system design and the detailed system design phases?

1012. Is there undesirable impact on staff or resources?

1013. How is agile program management done?

1014. Is there sufficient funding available for this?

1015. Who are the Automation Readiness project stakeholders?

1016. Is there adequate validation on required fields?

1017. How is agile portfolio management done?

1018. What resources (both financial and non-financial) are available/needed?

1019. How were collaborations developed, and how are they sustained?

1020. How is Agile Automation Readiness project Management done?

1021. Overall, how does the program function to serve the clients?

1022. Use: how will they use the information?

1023. What departments are involved in its daily operation?

1024. Where is the Risk in the Automation Readiness project?

1025. Do clients benefit (change) from the services?

4.1 Project Performance Report: Automation Readiness

1026. To what degree is there centralized control of information sharing?

1027. To what degree does the informal organization make use of individual resources and meet individual needs?

1028. How can Automation Readiness project sustainability be maintained?

1029. To what degree can team members vigorously define the teams purpose in considerations with others who are not part of the functioning team?

1030. What is the degree to which rules govern information exchange between groups?

1031. To what degree will new and supplemental skills be introduced as the need is recognized?

1032. How is the data used?

1033. To what degree are the goals realistic?

1034. To what degree can team members meet frequently enough to accomplish the teams ends?

1035. Next Steps?

1036. To what degree do individual skills and abilities

match task demands?

1037. What is in it for you?

1038. To what degree are the demands of the task compatible with and converge with the mission and functions of the formal organization?

1039. To what degree does the team possess adequate membership to achieve its ends?

1040. To what degree do team members feel that the purpose of the team is important, if not exciting?

1041. To what degree can the team ensure that all members are individually and jointly accountable for the teams purpose, goals, approach, and work-products?

4.2 Variance Analysis: Automation Readiness

1042. Are material costs reported within the same period as that in which BCWP is earned for that material?

1043. Are significant decision points, constraints, and interfaces identified as key milestones?

1044. Who is generally responsible for monitoring and taking action on variances?

1045. How are variances affected by multiple material and labor categories?

1046. Are the bases and rates for allocating costs from each indirect pool consistently applied?

1047. Are records maintained to show how management reserves are used?

1048. Are there knowledgeable Automation Readiness projections of future performance?

1049. Are work packages assigned to performing organizations?

1050. When, during the last four quarters, did a primary business event occur causing a fluctuation?

1051. How do you evaluate the impact of schedule changes, work around, et?

1052. What business event caused the fluctuation?

1053. What business event causes fluctuations?

1054. Do you identify potential or actual budget-based and time-based schedule variances?

1055. Is the market likely to continue to grow at this rate next year?

1056. Are overhead costs budgets established on a basis consistent with the anticipated direct business base?

1057. Are the wbs and organizational levels for application of the Automation Readiness projected overhead costs identified?

1058. Are all budgets assigned to control accounts?

1059. Do the rates and prices remain constant throughout the year?

4.3 Earned Value Status: Automation Readiness

1060. What is the unit of forecast value?

1061. Verification is a process of ensuring that the developed system satisfies the stakeholders agreements and specifications; Are you building the product right? What do you verify?

1062. Are you hitting your Automation Readiness projects targets?

1063. When is it going to finish?

1064. If earned value management (EVM) is so good in determining the true status of a Automation Readiness project and Automation Readiness project its completion, why is it that hardly any one uses it in information systems related Automation Readiness projects?

1065. Validation is a process of ensuring that the developed system will actually achieve the stakeholders desired outcomes; Are you building the right product? What do you validate?

1066. Where is evidence-based earned value in your organization reported?

1067. Where are your problem areas?

1068. How does this compare with other Automation

Readiness projects?

1069. How much is it going to cost by the finish?

1070. Earned value can be used in almost any Automation Readiness project situation and in almost any Automation Readiness project environment. it may be used on large Automation Readiness projects, medium sized Automation Readiness projects, tiny Automation Readiness projects (in cut-down form), complex and simple Automation Readiness projects and in any market sector. some people, of course, know all about earned value, they have used it for years - but perhaps not as effectively as they could have?

4.4 Risk Audit: Automation Readiness

1071. Who is responsible for what?

1072. Does your auditor understand your business?

1073. If applicable; are compilers and code generators available and suitable for the product to be built?

1074. Are formal technical reviews part of this process?

1075. Are staff committed for the duration of the product?

1076. Are all participants informed of safety issues?

1077. If applicable; does the software interface with new or unproven hardware or unproven vendor products?

1078. Is the number of people on the Automation Readiness project team adequate to do the job?

1079. When your organization is entering into a major contract, does it seek legal advice?

1080. Do you have position descriptions for all key paid and volunteer positions in your organization?

1081. Will safety checks of personal equipment supplied by competitors be conducted?

1082. Are auditors able to effectively apply more soft

evidence found in the risk-assessment process with the results of more tangible audit evidence found through more substantive testing?

1083. Auditor independence: a burdensome constraint or a core value?

1084. What are the boundaries of the auditors responsibility for policing management fidelity?

1085. Is safety information provided to all involved?

1086. Are your rules, by-laws and practices non-discriminatory?

1087. Is the customer technically sophisticated in the product area?

1088. What are the costs associated with late delivery or a defective product?

1089. If applicable; which route/packaging option do you choose for transport of hazmat material?

1090. Do you promote education and training opportunities?

4.5 Contractor Status Report: Automation Readiness

1091. Are there contractual transfer concerns?

1092. What process manages the contracts?

1093. What was the budget or estimated cost for your organizations services?

1094. What is the average response time for answering a support call?

1095. What was the overall budget or estimated cost?

1096. What are the minimum and optimal bandwidth requirements for the proposed solution?

1097. Who can list a Automation Readiness project as organization experience, your organization or a previous employee of your organization?

1098. What was the final actual cost?

1099. How is risk transferred?

1100. If applicable; describe your standard schedule for new software version releases. Are new software version releases included in the standard maintenance plan?

1101. How does the proposed individual meet each requirement?

1102. Describe how often regular updates are made to the proposed solution. Are corresponding regular updates included in the standard maintenance plan?

1103. What was the actual budget or estimated cost for your organizations services?

1104. How long have you been using the services?

4.6 Formal Acceptance: Automation Readiness

1105. Have all comments been addressed?

1106. What is the Acceptance Management Process?

1107. Does it do what client said it would?

1108. Was the Automation Readiness project work done on time, within budget, and according to specification?

1109. Did the Automation Readiness project manager and team act in a professional and ethical manner?

1110. Was the Automation Readiness project goal achieved?

1111. How does your team plan to obtain formal acceptance on your Automation Readiness project?

1112. Was the Automation Readiness project managed well?

1113. What features, practices, and processes proved to be strengths or weaknesses?

1114. Do you perform formal acceptance or burn-in tests?

1115. Did the Automation Readiness project achieve its MOV?

1116. Does it do what Automation Readiness project team said it would?

1117. Was the client satisfied with the Automation Readiness project results?

1118. How well did the team follow the methodology?

1119. What lessons were learned about your Automation Readiness project management methodology?

1120. Was business value realized?

1121. Who supplies data?

1122. What function(s) does it fill or meet?

1123. Do you buy-in installation services?

1124. General estimate of the costs and times to complete the Automation Readiness project?

5.0 Closing Process Group: Automation Readiness

1125. If a risk event occurs, what will you do?

1126. Were risks identified and mitigated?

1127. How well did the chosen processes produce the expected results?

1128. What could have been improved?

1129. Did the delivered product meet the specified requirements and goals of the Automation Readiness project?

1130. Is there a clear cause and effect between the activity and the lesson learned?

1131. Did the Automation Readiness project management methodology work?

1132. How will staff learn how to use the deliverables?

1133. Can the lesson learned be replicated?

1134. What were the actual outcomes?

1135. What is the overall risk of the Automation Readiness project to your organization?

1136. Did you do things well?

1137. What do you need to do?

1138. What went well?

1139. How well did the team follow the chosen processes?

1140. What were things that you need to improve?

1141. Are there funding or time constraints?

1142. When will the Automation Readiness project be done?

5.1 Procurement Audit: Automation Readiness

1143. Does your organization use existing contracts where possible to avoid the cost of bidding?

1144. If the expert was allowed to submit a tender, was all the relevant information the expert had gained from his earlier involvement made available to the other bidders?

1145. Has a deputy treasurer been appointed to sign checks when the treasurer is unable to perform that duty?

1146. Are advance payments to employees properly authorized and controlled?

1147. Is the strategy implemented across the entire organization?

1148. Are there procedures governing how sales and use tax will be handled (ordering in state versus ordering out of state)?

1149. Are information technology resources (e-procurement) used to reduce costs?

1150. Is there no evidence that the expert has influenced the decisions taken by the public authority in his/her interest or in the interest of a specific contractor?

1151. Are there performance targets on value for money obtained and cost savings?

1152. Are approval limits covered in written procedures?

1153. Does your organization have an administrative timetable to assist the staff in implementing the budget calendar?

1154. Are the rules for automatic payment in computer programs approved by management prior to implementation?

1155. Are services/tasks combined in such a way that the market is used where relevant?

1156. Is it tested periodically, whether your organizations way of handling tasks is competitive in relation to price and quality?

1157. Was the admissibility of variants displayed in the contract notice?

1158. If a purchase order calls for a cost-plus agreement, is the method of determining how final charges will be determined specified?

1159. Is there an effective risk management system continuously monitoring procurement risk?

1160. When corresponding references were made, was a precise description of the performance not otherwise possible and were the already stated references accompanied by the words or equivalent?

1161. Is the efficiency of the procurement process regularly evaluated?

1162. Does the procurement process compile basic procurement information such as how much is bought and spend with individual suppliers?

5.2 Contract Close-Out: Automation Readiness

1163. How is the contracting office notified of the automatic contract close-out?

1164. Parties: who is involved?

1165. What is capture management?

1166. Why Outsource?

1167. Has each contract been audited to verify acceptance and delivery?

1168. Have all acceptance criteria been met prior to final payment to contractors?

1169. Change in knowledge?

1170. Was the contract sufficiently clear so as not to result in numerous disputes and misunderstandings?

1171. Change in circumstances?

1172. Have all contract records been included in the Automation Readiness project archives?

1173. Change in attitude or behavior?

1174. What happens to the recipient of services?

1175. Have all contracts been completed?

1176. How does it work?

1177. Was the contract complete without requiring numerous changes and revisions?

1178. Have all contracts been closed?

1179. How/when used ?

1180. Are the signers the authorized officials?

1181. Parties: Authorized?

1182. Was the contract type appropriate?

5.3 Project or Phase Close-Out: Automation Readiness

1183. What was the preferred delivery mechanism?

1184. What could be done to improve the process?

1185. Planned remaining costs?

1186. Complete yes or no?

1187. What was expected from each stakeholder?

1188. Who exerted influence that has positively affected or negatively impacted the Automation Readiness project?

1189. In preparing the Lessons Learned report, should it reflect a consensus viewpoint, or should the report reflect the different individual viewpoints?

1190. Which changes might a stakeholder be required to make as a result of the Automation Readiness project?

1191. Does the lesson educate others to improve performance?

1192. Was the schedule met?

1193. How often did each stakeholder need an update?

1194. Have business partners been involved extensively, and what data was required for them?

1195. What is this stakeholder expecting?

1196. How much influence did the stakeholder have over others?

1197. Were cost budgets met?

1198. What hierarchical authority does the stakeholder have in your organization?

1199. What is the information level of detail required for each stakeholder?

1200. Who is responsible for award close-out?

5.4 Lessons Learned: Automation Readiness

1201. What is the distribution of authority?

1202. What is the economic growth rate?

1203. What would you approach differently next time?

1204. Was the change control process properly implemented to manage changes to cost, scope, schedule, or quality?

1205. How closely did deliverables match what was defined within the Automation Readiness project Scope?

1206. What were the main bottlenecks on the process?

1207. How long did redeployment take?

1208. What are the Benefits of Measurements?

1209. Are there any data that you have overlooked in identifying lessons?

1210. What specialization does the task require?

1211. What were the most significant issues on this Automation Readiness project?

1212. What are the internal fiscal constraints?

1213. How will you allocate your funding resources?

1214. If issue escalation was required, how effectively were issues resolved?

1215. What is the frequency of personal communications?

1216. Was the necessary hardware, software, accommodation etc available?

1217. How effective was the documentation that you received with the Automation Readiness project product/service?

1218. How extensive is middle management?

1219. How useful was the content of the training you received in preparation for the use of the product/service?

Index

266

control 2, 32, 53, 67, 80, 91-95, 97, 101-102, 126, 139, 146, 151, 154, 167, 173, 178, 209, 214, 217-218, 222, 238, 241, 259
controlled   68, 152, 195, 234, 252
controls   21, 62-63, 85, 89, 92-93, 95, 97, 99, 101, 137, 162
convention   111
converge   239
conversion   147
convey   1
convince   188
cooperate   177
Copyright   1
correct 44, 91
correction   151
corrective   51, 94, 152
correspond   9, 11
cosmetic   147
costing 57, 175
cost-plus   253
counsel   208
counter   131
counting   139
course 35, 58, 243
covered   253
covering   9, 99
coworker   112
create 11, 25, 61, 106, 112
created   69-70, 92, 125, 129, 132, 135, 168, 173, 191, 203, 210
creating   7, 45
creative   24
creativity   87
credible   177
crisis   26
criteria 2, 5, 9, 11, 34-35, 73, 88-89, 96, 105, 117, 124, 141, 143, 168, 177, 207, 255
CRITERION   2, 17, 29, 44, 59, 75, 91, 104
critical 32, 41, 70, 79, 92, 98, 115, 137, 147, 153, 155, 159, 167, 188, 214, 221, 232
criticism   . 69
crucial 72, 159, 168, 214
crystal 13
culture 42, 73, 201

resolved   171, 214, 229, 260
resource   3-4, 121, 125, 157-158, 163, 165-166, 191, 215
resources   2, 9, 22, 24, 26, 32, 34, 53, 73, 80, 92, 94, 111, 115,
121, 126, 132, 135, 145, 156, 161, 165, 170, 172-174, 177, 227,
233-234, 236, 238, 252, 260
respect   1
respective   132
respond   197, 229
responded   13
response   17, 26, 94, 97, 100, 207, 212, 246
responses   208
responsive   169, 178
restrict 142
result   70, 78, 137, 177, 180, 193, 219, 230, 255, 257
resulted   96
resulting   67, 136
results 9, 31-32, 66, 75-77, 82, 84, 89, 93, 102, 132-133, 167, 172,
177, 188, 207, 214, 223, 233, 245, 249-250
Retain 104
retained   62
retention   48
return   78, 118, 186
revenue   27, 56
revenues   55
review 11-12, 39, 64, 161, 171, 174-175, 179, 183, 210, 222, 228
reviewed   40, 205
Reviewer   233
reviews11, 145, 148, 162, 174, 188, 191, 206, 233, 244
revised 63, 96
revisions   256
revisit   221
reward 45-46, 66, 215
rewarded   27
rewards   102
rework 49, 53
rights   1
routine 100
rushing 234
safety   110, 224, 244-245
sample 207
satisfied   139, 226, 249
satisfies 242
satisfying   115

CPSIA information can be obtained
at www.ICGtesting.com
Printed in the USA
BVHW081414250719
554363BV00016B/1619/P